PRAISE FOR *HOT, SOUR, SALTY, SWEET*

"Su's wide-ranging interests as a writer unafraid of mingling flavors are evident throughout the book . . . Seasoned with a dash of her meticulously crafted poetry and even a recipe, this collection celebrates words, culture, food, and the human act of making that binds them all together. A literary gourmand's delight."
—*Kirkus Reviews*

"As an admirer of Adrienne Su's poems, I couldn't wait to read her debut essay collection. Sure enough, *Hot, Sour, Salty, Sweet* contains everything I love about Su's poems: warmhearted honesty, hyper-clear articulation, and a Frostian lump in the throat. Su tells us, 'cooking a meal, like writing a poem, is an act of making.' At their core such acts, she demonstrates, are the same. Her essays move organically from poetics to cookbooks, Maxine Kumin to Julia Child, sestinas to General Tso's Chicken. Reading *Hot, Sour, Salty, Sweet* is like having a great conversation with a brilliant poet-friend as they prepare a beautiful meal."
—John Wall Barger, author of *Smog Mother*

"Adrienne Su's *Hot, Sour, Salty, Sweet* is a fragrant weave of essays, remembrances, interviews with writer-mentors, and poems (even a recipe or two). Complex nuances are rendered on the page as well as on the tongue (through all the senses, actually). Her Middle Kingdom is a home in the suburban south, where memories of

frozen pizza, mac and cheese, and mashed potatoes share equal space with dumplings, Cantonese roast pork, and pickled vegetables. Here are thoughtful and generous tributes to the many kindred forms of creative making—for one thing, there is what the poet does with language and writing; for another, there is what daughter/mother/teacher stirs together and serves up at the table, for sustenance as well as insight and empowerment."
—Luisa A. Igloria, author of *Maps for Migrants and Ghosts*

"The essays in Adrienne Su's *Hot, Sour, Salty, Sweet* illuminate the poet's journey from the south of her childhood where 'there was no language for addressing what made me different' to Harvard University where she began to parse her relationship to Chinese culture, language, and food. They move through time (the first was written in 1996) and allow the reader a glimpse into the evolution of a major American poet. Along the way we learn about her sense of kinship with the poet Adrienne Rich, with whom she shares 'poetry, feminism, motherhood, the quest for identity.' Su discovers a passion for cooking and struggles with 'the dim view that artists and intellectuals tend to take of cookbooks.' Su is honest and intellectually curious and willing to hold two opposing viewpoints at the same time. This volume is an important companion to her poems."
—Faith Shearin, author of *The Owl Question* and *Lost Language*, and 2022 nonfiction winner of The Perkoff Prize

HOT, SOUR, SALTY, SWEET

The author in her kitchen

Hot, Sour, Salty, Sweet

Essays and Interviews

Adrienne Su

pcb

PAUL DRY BOOKS
Philadelphia 2024

First Paul Dry Books Edition, 2024

Paul Dry Books, Inc.
Philadelphia, Pennsylvania
www.pauldrybooks.com

Printed in the United States of America

Library of Congress Control Number: 2024939326
ISBN 9781589881921

Table of Contents

5: INTERVIEWS AND A FEW POEMS

ACKNOWLEDGMENTS

VERSIONS OF works in this volume previously appeared in *The Atlanta Journal-Constitution, Beard House, The Best American Poetry* blog, *Good Eats: 32 Writers on Eating Ethically, Four Way Review, A Gathering of the Tribes, Girls: An Anthology, The Hopkins Review, Mentor & Muse, New England Review Digital, New Ohio Review, Northwest Review, Prairie Schooner, Saveur,* and *VIDA: Women in Literary Arts.*

The poems "Substitutions" and "That Almond Dessert" first appeared in *New England Review*; "An Hour Later, You're Hungry Again" in *The New Yorker*; and "Wedding Gifts" in *Indiana Review.*

I am indebted not only to the editors of these publications and the interviewers included here but also to my longtime readers of work in progress, Jennifer Joseph, Sharon O'Brien, Faith Shearin, and Melanie Sumner, and to everyone at Paul Dry Books. I am grateful, also, to Dickinson College (especially for the insights of my amazing colleagues), the Mellon Foundation, Vermont Studio Center, Virginia Center for the Creative Arts, and Yaddo, for essential support in the completion of this book.

Introduction

M Y MAIN GENRE, poetry, has a low page count relative to the number of days, weeks, or months spent writing. I'm a writer who habitually deletes most of what I write, and what survives tends to wind up corralled into a formal structure, using rhyme or at least stanzas. Every poem begins with a knot in the stomach, a gray area that resists linear modes of disentanglement. A successful poem dwells in that ambiguity and relies in large part on the music of its form to seek resolution.

Yet there are times when poetry is not the right approach for the knot I'm trying to untie. Sometimes I figure this out as I am attempting a poem, a string of thwarted drafts revealing that exploration will go better in an essay. I may need to make an argument, and not in the elliptical way in which a sonnet might make an argument. Or there is a pressing situation, such as the 2021 shootings in Atlanta-area spas, that calls for an immediate, direct response in a less specialized venue than the literary journals where I usually publish. Or I want to consider something about poetry that is best discussed in an expository mode. Or I'm visiting the alternate universe in which I became a food writer instead of a poet. For all these reasons and more, I have habitually written prose on occasion. This book gathers the prose pieces in which I believe I learned the most as I wrote.

Over many years of giving readings, I've also learned that the "prose" portion of a live poetry reading—the remarks the poet makes between poems—often makes a crucial difference in the audience's experience. A book launch usually draws non-poetry readers from the poet's family or community: people who come to show support but don't normally attend events like this. They sometimes expect to feel lost, but many have told me afterwards that the brief introduction I gave to contextualize each poem opened the poem's world and made the genre, at least in that moment, approachable. And even seasoned poetry people—fellow poets, scholars of poetry, readers of poetry—have expressed appreciation for the asides. It's not just novices who enjoy a bit of context.

This collection can be seen as those remarks on a larger scale—the conversational, "prose" side of my body of work so far. They are also a partial account of my journey to becoming a poet. To this end, I've arranged most essays in chronological order, with some exceptions: I've grouped together three pieces on the late Claire Kageyama-Ramakrishnan, about whom I wrote on three separate occasions, and the interview section is bookended by two poems that don't stick to chronology.

Although the majority of the pieces were written in the last decade, this collection spans a long time-frame, almost three decades. I have taken the liberty of including the voice of today in brief remarks at the beginning of each section of the book, for unity, clarity, and context. I have also kept the italicization of words I don't expect most readers to know (*guanxi*) but opted not to italicize others that have entered the common English lexicon in my lifetime (ramen). Opinions will differ on what should be italicized, and the status of some words will one day be different for the simple reason that language is alive and always changing. Like an émigré for whom the old country remains, fixed in memory, as it was upon the moment of departure, a piece of writing captures aspects of the temporal moment of its composition. In gathering these pieces, I have tried to strike a balance between the old and new sensibilities that make up the whole of this collection.

·1·

Origins: Cooking, Writing, Becoming

North South East West:
Notes on Section One

THE ESSAYS in this section tangle with presence and absence, often through the memory—mine or someone else's—of a place. "Codes of Conduct" considers the American South in which I grew up from the perspective of my first sustained absence from it. "Culinary Chauvinism" and "My Middle Kingdom" contemplate a China described by parents and grandparents to a younger generation that grew up never having touched its soil. "She, without Apology" addresses the scarcity of female voices in the history of literature in English, as well as their relative abundance in culinary writings. "Terse Wisdom, Casual, Not Lofty" recalls Charles Wright's classroom at the University of Virginia, nearly twenty years after I left Charlottesville, and "What's in a Name" invokes Adrienne Rich, whom I never met, on the grounds of her alma mater, Radcliffe College, which had merged with Harvard by the time I arrived there.

As M.F.K. Fisher famously (and rhetorically) asked, and as many literary writers have also asked since, Why do I write about food? For most of my adult life, cooking and writing have competed for hours in the day. This looks like a practical problem, but it's more complex than that: practical solutions to the question of dinner—meal kits, planning apps, high-quality prepared food—keep growing more abundant, yet the struggle continues. Since cooking a meal, like writing a poem, is an act of making, I can't resist contemplating its meaning even when I think I only want to get food on the table. The parallels between cooking and writing especially underlie "My Middle Kingdom" but energize much of this volume, particularly in section four.

A caveat: "She, without Apology" is a product of its time. The aspect of English usage—singular pronouns—that it addresses has changed since I wrote the essay in 2002. We are better for those changes, having broadly opted to acknowledge more than two gender identities by using the pronoun "they" with a plural verb and both plural and singular meanings. Since many of my personal circumstances have changed over the last two decades, I have opted not to reinvent the piece as if it had been written in 2023 but to view it as a snapshot of my reading life in 2002. As a result, the discussion of language is sometimes dated. The speed with which the piece has become an emblem of an earlier age is, I believe, a sign of hope.

Codes of Conduct

IN THE SOUTH, where I grew up, the people have an unspoken agreement: Reality is what everyone says it is. The agreement is meant to protect others from any perceived slight. It can be as innocuous as complimenting an ugly outfit, but among the truly polite, you could walk into church with a horse instead of your husband, and everyone would not only fail to notice anything wrong but also exclaim, "What a beautiful hat you have on! And Harry is looking so well! The two of you must come over for dinner sometime." By the end of the day, you'd actually believe that the horse was a man.

In the third grade, friends and I often re-enacted scenes from *Little House on the Prairie*. My blonde friend played Mary because of the color of her hair. Another played Carrie, the youngest sister, because she was the youngest. I played Laura, "because you have dark hair," the others explained. Nobody ever pointed out that I did not in the slightest resemble a white Midwestern girl with freckles and brown pigtails. (I was happy to oblige for another reason: Laura was the star of the series, the central character and a future author.) To suggest that perhaps I looked more like a long-lost daughter of a railroad worker of that time was to suggest that I looked different from my friends, and that simply was not done.

Not that the subject never came up—there might be a snack in my lunch that the other kids thought strange, or a teacher might discreetly ask about the trip my father took shortly after Nixon's visit opened China to the U.S. But most of the time, there was no language for addressing what made me different. No one asked me about Chinese culture or how to say things in Chinese, which I didn't know, anyway. Questions of the sort were considered rude, a way of pointing out that I looked Chinese, rather than the Southern gal I was.

This doesn't sound too serious—just a form of Southern gentility. But imagine living your whole life in an environment where everyone says that a cat is a dog, all the time. Your perception of animals changes. You see a cat racing up a tree and remark, "My, that dog is a good climber." You hear a plaintive meow from outside and put a beef bone in the backyard. And when you yourself are a cat in this world, you grow to think you are a dog.

This is fine until you leave this world—and go to a land known as the North, where people not only recognize cathood but celebrate it. They form alliances to preserve feline culture, holding fish dinners and mouse-catching lectures. They hold cat networking activities and cat social events—even writers' conferences for cats who have a way with words. For the cat who's lived her whole life thinking she's a dog, this can come as a bit of a shock.

Up North, I'd find myself in a group of Chinese Americans and think, Hey, I'm surrounded! before realizing that I blended in. I'd go to a gathering of Chinese students and wait to be discovered and thrown out. Talking with my Korean American roommate, I found that I wasn't the only one whose lack of interest in math and science was seen as a possible birth defect.

One day, when I referred to myself as "Oriental," everyone in the room—white, Korean, Hispanic—pounced on me.

"It's Asian," they cried. "Oriental is offensive."

That was how I learned that there was a vocabulary for a long-unnamed aspect of my life. My visceral feelings of family obligation were known as filial piety, or, as my roommate and I described it,

Asian guilt. My parents' unwillingness to contradict their friends was an act of saving face for all. And the melodramatic struggles to pay for dinner were not earnest fights but the desire to avoid *guanxi*, or obligation, to the other party.

I went home using not the big words of a kid home from college, but ordinary words for things that were familiar, in fact mundane, to my parents.

"I think we're making an unbalanced dinner," I said, peering into a beef stew. "Too many hot-element ingredients, too few cold elements. Maybe—"

My mother, absorbed in *The Wall Street Journal*, waved a dismissive hand. My father, opening his mail, murmured, "Whatever." My brother, who was getting ready for hockey practice, was already out the door.

The next evening, I visited my best friend, the one who'd played Carrie, and sat down to my zillionth Southern dinner with her family.

"What classes are you taking?" her mother asked.

"I'm taking Chinese, so I can eavesdrop on my parents," I said, "and a course in East Asian religions—"

"What kind of job do you plan to get with that?" my friend's father joked.

"I just want to know enough to be able to talk to my relatives in China," I said. "To find out who I really am."

What happened next was very strange. You could hear a crumb of cornbread drop. My friend's house had always been a second home to me, as mine was to her, but on this topic, her family, unlike mine, was stuck. And it was my fault: I had carelessly dragged the conversation into never-never land, the land of what made me different.

During that frozen silence, I busied myself eating. Then I heard myself say:

"These mashed potatoes are wonderful! I've been so homesick for them. Up North, people just don't know how to cook."

My friend's mother urged me to have more. My friend's father passed the gravy and made a joke about Yankees. And instantly, my friend and I were eight years old again and digging into our plates, ravenous as puppies, because we were growing so fast.

1996

Culinary Chauvinism

For sixteen of the last seventeen years, my parents took my grandparents out for dinner at least once a week, usually twice. This ritual began when I was eleven and my mother's parents moved from Taiwan to Atlanta, and it slowed down but did not stop last year, when my grandfather died.

When my grandparents moved to Atlanta, their annual visits, with gifts and much attention for the kids, were transformed into their continuous presence, which, by nature of being continuous, was not festive as in the old days. Since their ruling passion in life was to eat, however, my grandmother regularly donned brightly colored suits, her best jewelry, and red lipstick for our dinners out, whether we ate at a fancy restaurant or an all-you-can-eat cafeteria.

My grandfather talked endlessly about the food, often took pictures of it, and assigned each of us a favorite dish, accurately or not. He urged more on us all the time, in the manner of the Chinese host, even when he was not the host. Sometimes we secretly complained about his presumptuous grandiosity, but last fall, when it became clear that he was not going to survive his bout with pneumonia, my family and I sat around our dinner table and talked with rare nostalgia about his overflowing enthusiasm for eating. My father, who had been told weekly for sixteen years that he liked steamed fish, missed him already. My brother thought back to the evening when our grandfather had arbitrarily named Chicken with Asparagus my brother's dish, much to his irritation, and knew that Chicken with Asparagus would, in a way, become the dish associated with our grandfather.

Although they had a soft spot for steak and potatoes, my grandparents were sturdy devotees of Chinese food, particularly the foods of their native Shanghai and the surrounding region. They were tireless eaters of white-fleshed fish, usually sea bass or snapper, stunned to death just moments before and steamed with ginger, scallions, soy sauce, and Shaoxing wine until just opaque. They were great fans of the soup-filled dumplings of Suzhou and could bear the broth, which is normally hotter than its wrapper, at any temperature. Well into their eighties, they tore into crispy spring rolls like teenagers and deftly separated the fine bones from the flesh of *xunyu,* the chunky, smoky-flavored carp served cold as an appetizer in Shanghai-style restaurants. My grandmother, who is ninety this year and diligently watches her health, still has her gustatory enthusiasm intact.

As kids, my brother and I sometimes grew weary of eating in Chinese restaurants. All our lives, we had been taken to them frequently, and although we were great fans of suburban Mongolian Beef and General Tso's Chicken, we sometimes wanted a change, or just to stay home. Our best friends, also a sister and brother, came from a family who did not own a wok. They ate breaded cube steak, fried chicken, and boiled turnip greens, and we were often invited to join them. While we found their food perfectly normal and frequently ate Southern-style meals in our own house, we knew that they found our food less normal than we found theirs, and like all kids, we were aware of our difference and wished to minimize it. We had seen the elderly woman next door, upon bringing us peas from her garden, refuse my mother's offer to cook some Chinese-style so that she might try a new taste. "No, thank you," she said sweetly, "I like 'em the way I've always cooked 'em." We had learned not to bring Chinese snacks to school, where other kids held their noses and said, "Gross! What are you eating?"

Because we knew of our culinary marginality, we were sometimes disappointed, although not surprised, when our parents asked our grandparents where they would like to eat, got a gentle "Anywhere will be fine," pressed them for a stronger opinion, and got another gentle reply: "Anywhere, we'll eat anything. Cantonese *or* Shanghainese."

In the restaurant, the two of us of had a separate conversation while our elders held an impassioned discussion of the menu. The waiters knew, as they had not known in the '70s, that they could not expect the young people to understand Chinese. They brought us ice water almost automatically, while the adults sipped hot tea. We were bored most of the time and excluded from the adult conversation, which often involved bumping into Chinese American friends in the restaurant. Still, complaining or not, we enjoyed our Chinese food as much as our Southern food and went home well stuffed.

What we could not understand—and what I still, to some degree, do not understand—was our grandparents' inability ever to tire of Chinese food. Although they did not eat it exclusively, they were quite capable of doing so, even in this land of great variety, and we could not see why. Didn't they crave a plain roast chicken sometimes? Or warm peach cobbler with cream, or a grilled-cheese sandwich? To us, Chinese food, although good, was just another category of food, and if you ate it all the time, you condemned yourself to certain boredom. It occurred to us that people in China probably ate Chinese food all the time, but they didn't count, as they didn't have the opportunity to eat mashed potatoes, sharp cheddar cheese, Caesar salad, and other glories of the Western table.

For many years, I thought my grandparents were making a terrible mistake, closing themselves off from many avenues of dining pleasure, which was clearly their favorite form of pleasure. As Atlanta grew more cosmopolitan and I learned more about food, I wondered why they didn't go to Thai or Korean restaurants, or French or Italian ones. During college, on visits home, I dragged my family to every kind of restaurant but Chinese, as much to try them myself as to get them interested. "Let's go by ourselves," my parents usually said, once I had convinced them to go. "Grandma and Grandpa won't be able to take it."

So maybe it was their age, I concluded, and gave up trying to fight nature, at least as the two of them were concerned.

As it turned out, it would have been a losing battle with the rest of the family, too, which was beginning to grow more Chinese. Every year, another cousin appeared at the Atlanta airport with a single suitcase and twenty to thirty words of English. They were from my father's family, most of whom I had never met, and China was just beginning to open up to the West. My parents housed my cousins in the guest bedroom for a few months, then enrolled them in graduate schools and found them apartments. The supply of relatives, all adults, seemed endless, and they were all in the sciences or engineering, always my worst subjects.

While my Chinese cousins, freshly arrived, were remote from me and my brother, so remote that the dinner-table dichotomy continued at home, they had an immediate impact on holiday meals. Always eager to help, they responded to our invitations to Thanksgiving dinner by swamping our kitchen with homemade specialties, doubling the already abundant spread and, to the distress of my brother and me, Sinicizing Thanksgiving.

Roast turkey arrived marinated in soy sauce and sherry. Stuffing was replaced with *lao mian*, or fried noodles with seafood and vegetables, and *chaofan*, fried rice with minced meats, eggs, small shrimp, peas, and mushrooms. Instead of a platter of steamed Brussels sprouts or a corn souffle, there was a platter of stir-fried Chinese broccoli, perhaps seasoned with garlic and oyster sauce.

There were mountains of homemade spring rolls, lightly browned fried turnip cakes, and a clear soup in which floated delicate meat dumplings with wrinkly, transparent wrappers. All of this went on the table next to the honeyed ham, sweet potatoes, cranberry sauce, mashed potatoes, gravy, and pecan and pumpkin pies. Everyone took a plate and circled the table. It would be easy to guess who ate what.

It was an increasingly typical American holiday, the new immigrant fare mixing with the established, but I found it disturbingly self-contradictory. The flavors of Thanksgiving were, to my mind, fixed by a kind of sanctity. You could change your turkey stuffing each year, or add cardamom to the sweet potatoes, or substitute apple pie for the pecan. But you could not eat *lao mian* as stuffing for your turkey—absolutely not. It was un-American. Nervous about dairy products, some of the guests did not dare put cream or ice cream on their pie, and for some reason, this made me very angry. What right had anyone to misinterpret the foods of Thanksgiving, to celebrate it with red-cooked shrimp, to smother an American cornucopia with fried turnip cakes?

It was not that I did not like the food they brought; it was beautiful food, made from scratch with the meticulous diligence and respect for ingredients that the first-generation immigrant brings to a country that's been spoiled by abundance. The problem was that it somehow missed the point; it did not spring from the story of the continent, the Pilgrims arriving at the astonishing New World, the Native Americans offering their knowledge of the flora and fauna, even the turkey almost becoming our national bird. It seemed to me disrespectful of American history to gather and celebrate our good fortune with all the wrong foods. Any other day, these foods would be fine, were in fact an important contribution to the country's culinary life, but on Thanksgiving, they were out of place. It was like thanking the wrong land.

As they settled into jobs and marriages and started having American children of their own, my cousins became more American, at least in the predictable sense. Raised under Communism, they became capitalist success stories. They learned to speak and write fine English. They live in neat suburbs and apartment complexes, maintain their lawns and gardens, drive everywhere, and give their children English names. But drop in on them at dinnertime any evening, and you are most likely to find the table spread with Chinese food. They will urge you to sit down, quickly setting a place for you with a bowl of rice, a small plate, and a pair of chopsticks. They will pile up your bowl with shrimp and snow peas, duck in red-wine sediment paste, fried oysters, and stir-fried greens from the garden.

I used to think of their devotion to Chinese food as resistance to assimilation, an unwillingness to try new things, but now I think they are simply changing the landscape of American cooking. There is no reason why the cooking techniques of Fuzhou, China, combined with ingredients grown in Georgia, should not make another American food. Alongside their tomato plants, my relatives grow several kinds of "Chinese" squash and leafy greens in their gardens, gardens nourished by Georgia soil, Georgia sunshine, and Georgia rain. The seeds may have come from abroad, but so did the first seeds of that fruit by which the state of Georgia identifies itself, the peach. (Incidentally, it's of Chinese origin—and all squashes come from the Americas.) My cousins are nurturing and eating from the American earth, the same as the European and African immigrants before them.

Pumpkin pie does not evoke the same emotions in them that it evokes in me—although I imagine that they feel something for it when they are in China, visiting, and no one around them has an opinion about pumpkin pie—except, perhaps, that it must be bad, because Western food is so universally dismissed as inferior there, mainly by people who have never eaten it. Their beloved foods are still the foods of their childhoods, of their parents and grandparents. To give them up would be like my giving up pie on Thanksgiving: unimaginable. They may be chauvinistic about Fuzhou-style cooking, just as my grandparents were about Shanghai-style, but they have shown me that I have my patriotisms, too.

Lucky enough to have grown up with more than one cuisine, I am happy eating in both the East and the West, but because I am passionate about both, I become homesick wherever I must eat only one, and defensive when either is attacked. When I lived in China, for instance, I always wanted to get my hands on a pizza. When living in the Blue Ridge Mountains in Virginia, I could only dream that a dim-sum cart was rolling by. When someone I met in Ireland told me, apologetically, that she didn't like Chinese food, that helpless, mute sense of protest came up in my throat—that useless feeling you get when you want to explain a significant dream that falls flat in the telling, or when you are trying to win someone over who long ago decided not to believe your side of the story. The same feeling struck in China, where a young man lectured me on Western food being a primitive matter of boiling large chunks of meat and butchering them at the table. Neither critic had been to any of the lands whose foods they were dismissing, and neither had had the opportunity to experience those foods properly anywhere, yet one could not argue the point with words alone. It is hard to convert a newcomer to the appreciation of a taste experience without the context of local ingredients, honest cooking, the smell of the air and earth that formed it, and the company of people who understand it. Most of the time it is impossible to convert anyone to foods they are prejudiced against or suspicious of. And finally, after all, it is a personal matter that begins with the foods of one's childhood. I wish I could make everyone understand my love for the mixed-up foods of my corner of America—the southeastern corner, which contains my grandfather's ashes and my cousins' gardens—but even in my increasingly omnivorous enthusiasm I am every bit as opinionated as the next person, so I suppose it is only fair to leave other people's gastronomic passions and hatreds alone, to eat and let eat, as my family does on Thanksgiving, to accept certain limitations of understanding so that all may live and dine in peace.

1996

My Middle Kingdom

IT HAS HAPPENED again. My guests are sitting back, well-stuffed and tipsy. I have pulled off a proper Chinese dinner, from the crackling pan of pot stickers to the whole steamed fish, and I'm trying not to look surprised.

Someone asks, "Where did you learn to cook?"

I fidget, then say a bit too fast, "From my mother."

It is not exactly a lie. My mother spent much of my childhood preparing meals both Chinese and Western, and sometimes I helped wrap the wonton or toss the salad. Most of the time, however, she cooked while I played or read, and when dinner was ready, I came to eat it, usually with a book in hand.

"From my mother," however, is still the correct answer. It evokes images of a daughter and her pioneer mother in a '70s Atlanta kitchen, then the mother as a girl in a '40s Shanghai kitchen with her mother, and so on—generation after generation of women handing down culinary wisdom, from Chinese antiquity to this afternoon in 1998, as I stand in my Cape Cod kitchen, scrubbing mussels that are about to meet their maker in a bath of sherry, ginger, and fermented black beans. Perhaps it goes all the way back to a man, the Song Dynasty poet and gourmet Su Dongpo, whom some of my relatives like to claim as an ancestor, and after whom a famous dish of braised pork, Dongpo Rou, was named.

Such notions suggest that the dinner that has just been consumed is the real thing, not some washed-out American version of ginger beef or phoenix-tail shrimp, because I have genetic license to prepare it properly.

This is how I used to feel about my Chineseness in general, that it was passed down biologically, like the color of my hair and eyes, and that I had a kind of automatic passport into Chinese society, should I ever wish to join it. Although I had been born in Georgia Baptist Hospital, couldn't speak Chinese, and did not set foot in Asia until I was nineteen, I had grown up in a community that considered me Chinese, so I thought I was. My parents had become U.S. citizens before I was born, but they did not mind being called "Chinese" or even "Oriental"; they had grown up in China and tended to use the word "American" to mean "white American." If someone referred to Chinese food as "exotic," it was fair enough, because once upon a time, mashed potatoes had been "exotic" to them.

For the children, however, the terms used to describe us suggested that we were not American. I think it was sometime after we had reached our adult heights and weights that it first occurred to us to wonder what this meant we were, what "Chinese" meant. From the way people treated us, we could gather this much: We were math-and-science whizzes; we played musical instruments well; we valued hard work; we were soft-spoken and studious. Also: We weren't the best literature students; we were not creative; we bound women's feet; and we ate dogs.

People also assumed that in a Chinese restaurant, we knew what to order. That was perhaps the one respect in which they were right.

I grew up in suburbia, at a time when the women were shifting from being full-time housewives to being mothers with outside careers. They tried to maintain pristine homes and happy families while working forty hours a week, invariably for less than they were worth and far below their creative and intellectual potential.

Like each family's neat green lawn, menus were predictable from house to house: spaghetti with sauce from a jar, iceberg lettuce salad perked up with dressing from a bottle, chicken baked with breading from a box. Convenience was the culinary cutting edge, and a kid's lunch bag did not meet the schoolyard standard unless it included a vacuum-sealed juice pack or at least an individual bag of chips—proof that their mothers had better things to do than wash thermoses and distribute potato chips into sandwich bags.

My family depended on these standbys just like our neighbors, but we also had a second set of standbys. These included Cantonese roast pork, which my mother made in quantity and froze; dried somen noodles, which we boiled up in canned chicken broth with sliced Napa cabbage; and a pantry full of pickled vegetables made by my aunt, who often visited from Savannah. Also, we had Chinese American family friends, addressed by my brother and me as "Aunties" and "Uncles," who turned up with homemade spring rolls, fried noodles, and whole fish ready for steaming. One Auntie became known to us as "the snail-bun lady" for her plain steamed buns, sprinkled with sesame oil and scallions, that were coiled like big white snail shells. Another brought trays full of homemade meat dumplings, ready to freeze, boil, or pan-fry.

My mother, who was raised in a Shanghai house with a cook, had learned how to cook in America because it was expected of her, and because she was hungry. Thus her culinary knowledge, Eastern and Western, came from books written in English, and from the cooks among the Aunties.

My parents' friendships with the Aunties and Uncles dated back to the early 1960s, when one couldn't buy tofu or wonton wrappers in Atlanta. They had made their own tofu then, starting with mail-order soybeans and plaster of Paris. They kneaded and formed their own dumpling and spring-roll skins; they sprouted mung beans at home. These were the opposite of convenience foods; these were the foods they craved and would go to great lengths to taste again. They did the work not because they enjoyed it or wanted to save the planet, but because they were hungry.

As a teenager, I knew I wanted to be a writer. I read and wrote without considering the genre barriers that would trouble me later: stories, poems, essays, a try at a young-adult novel. In my bedroom, the world seemed to be emerging on blank sheets of paper, and I couldn't wait to enter it.

Later, in college up North, I began studying Chinese civilization and learning Mandarin from scratch, out of two personal hungers, one for a body of knowledge less Eurocentric than the one offered in high school, one for stories that might give gravity and purpose to my poetry and fiction.

It seemed that Chinese history was something I should know, especially since it seemed to contain my family's history. I thought that if my writing were to have urgency and moral weight, it would address—or at least possess awareness of—what my predecessors had experienced during the Chinese civil wars and wars with Japan, the Great Leap Forward, the Cultural Revolution, and other twentieth-century upheavals. In 1979, when I was twelve, my father had made his first trip back to his hometown in Fujian since 1949—a fact I liked to cite at school because it made the teachers gasp. I watched my father pack a suitcase with mountains of ballpoint pens, neon Frisbees, and bright skeins of wool. Why is he taking such common stuff? I wondered, and tried to imagine a country without pens.

With the snippets of information my parents had given, casually, over the years, I formed a foggy picture. The Japanese had invaded when my father was a youth; when I asked what he had seen, he had said neutrally, "Atrocities." My mother, as a girl in Shanghai, had stepped over the frozen bodies of the Asian and Caucasian homeless. My father had had a brother and a sister who didn't survive into adulthood, due to ailments that would be easily treatable now.

My mother's family had had a beloved dog, who, left in the care of friends when the family fled for Taiwan, died apparently of a broken heart. My father's family, when insects got into their rice, spent all day picking the insects out rather than waste the grain. And one day, when our basement flooded, my mother was forced to take all her Chinese dresses out of their storage bags: custom-tailored qipaos in muted blues, pinks, reds, and yellows, ruined by water, signifiers of a whole other life.

Wanting the full picture, I studied Chinese history, literature, mythology, thought, and language, and just before my junior year in college, got what I thought I needed most, a scholarship to study in Shanghai for a year.

That fall, I moved into Fudan University's Foreign Students' Compound, a severe, heavily guarded complex containing dorms, classrooms, and a dining room for foreigners and a handful of government-appointed Chinese roommates, who kept tabs on us. It should not have been surprising that the dining room served Chinese food three times a day, but it seemed a fabulous treat to me. Back in Cambridge, the best approximation of Chinese food in the dorms had been the occasional stir-fry that happened to contain soy sauce and a few snow peas. Real Chinese food in college was reserved for dates and night-before-the-exam takeout. There was something novel and indulgent about having it all the time, and unlike most of my classmates, I didn't get lonely for another kind of food for many weeks.

My first real Chinese conversation in Shanghai took place near the university, with a fruit vendor.

"Where are you from?" the vendor, a middle-aged man, asked.

"America, but my mother's family home is in Shanghai," I said.

"Ah, you've come back," he said, filling a newsprint bag with yellow pears. He smiled, revealing black gaps between his teeth. "Welcome home."

"Thank you," I said, and paid him.

Back in the compound, I followed all the guidebook warnings and washed and peeled the first pear carefully. It was firm and juicy and peeled easily, but when I cut into it, it revealed itself to be rotten inside. The next pear was rotten, too; so was the next. Every pear was rotten, and later I realized I had also paid triple the normal price.

All over China that year, I seemed to get the equivalent of rotten pears. "She doesn't really know how to use chopsticks," someone commented at a dinner table. "You write like a foreigner; what's wrong with you?" a teacher asked after reading an essay I had written in elementary Chinese. "You aren't a real foreigner," my Chinese roommate said, "but you aren't a real Chinese person, either." (The word for "foreigner" tended to mean "white person" in conversation.) At the entrances to tourist hotels, guards gripped me by the arm until I produced my passport, after which they cowered; I don't know which reaction troubled me more. White American tourists looked through me, even while I conversed with them in their own English. Travel was a nightmare of standing in long lines and arguing with reluctant clerks. My foreign classmates, also frustrated with the Communist bureaucracy and their own physical and psychological isolation, railed bitterly against the Chinese, and I railed with them, yet felt evil and divided for doing so.

The country that had held such mythical stature in my mind annoyed me more than it moved me and welcomed mainly my dollars. I might as well have gone to Hungary or the Soviet Union. The neighbors back in Atlanta had been using the wrong terms all along. Nothing about me was at home in China.

What did move me was the private unrest of students who were beginning to stage protests, protests that would eventually build up to the cataclysmic one in Tiananmen Square in 1989. I could see History beginning to happen, even feel it in the streets sometimes, the same kind of History I was trying to grasp so that I might understand my parents' past lives. I could see why the contemporary literature, which disappointed me by being short on interior life, was political; life was political. I watched and listened; I met many relatives for the first time, and gave them pens and stockings.

Nevertheless, stories rarely came from firsthand sources; mainly, I got them from my parents in letters and over the phone.

Among our elders were a man who had been arbitrarily exiled to decades of poverty and loneliness in the countryside, a woman who was abused throughout her old age by cruel stepchildren, a woman whose husband had destroyed her psychologically after taking a young second wife.... All of this seemed to matter in a way that my own experiences—biking with my best friend to the Seven-Eleven for an Icee or attempting to teach my rebellious Welsh corgi to heel—seemed banal, unnecessary even.

In the spring of 1988, having traveled to several regions and become fairly fluent in Mandarin, I left China with the intention of telling the stories I now knew about the place, the impersonal ones of official corruption and crackdowns on political dissent as well as the personal ones of my own family's trials during the various revolts and revolutions.

Shortly after scenes from the massacre in Tiananmen Square flashed across our television screens, I graduated from college and took my first job and apartment, in New York City. Because the job was entry-level and in publishing, I was poor and likely to remain that way. I was writing poetry with sureness and ease, but to give expression to what I had recently learned, and also in the hope of making some money, I began writing a novel as well. Mornings before work, nights after work, and sometimes during lunch hour at work, I worked on chapters about a Chinese family that gradually reveals its shattering personal history to a visiting American relative. (*The Joy Luck Club* came out around this time; its success suggested that people were willing to listen to such a story, and gave me a greater sense of urgency.)

In the meantime, I had to figure out ways to stretch my sorry paycheck, most fundamentally by learning to cook. Although I had perhaps one frying pan and could not tell a raw chicken breast from a raw pork loin, I had hope. My apartment was a furnished sublet with a kitchen full of saucepans, dishes, and utensils, along with a bookshelf jammed with cookbooks. I began to cook from the apartment's fading Time-Life *Foods of the World* series and the other volumes that the owners had accumulated over the years, mainly classics like *The Joy of Cooking* and *The New York Times Cookbook*.

It turned out that I was as interested in cooking as I was in eating, and I wanted to know about every regional food covered by Time-Life, plus any regions they had missed. I tasted the real things at some of Manhattan's cheapest restaurants, many of which were around the corner. The Indian restaurants on Sixth Street, the Polish diners on First Avenue, and the Vietnamese noodle shops in Chinatown each offered entry into a universe of food. These places taught me things about cooking that I couldn't have learned from books. They were about styles of eating, which offered some insight into people, who must have been shaped by the same ecological forces that shaped their cuisines.

Each new dining experience, however humble, sent me into another flurry of culinary research, generally in bookstores, immigrant-run grocery stores, and Greenmarkets. When I wasn't writing, I was cooking, from whatever cuisine had most recently crossed my path. Friends and acquaintances, living on takeout, offered themselves up as guinea pigs.

What mystified me was that my Chinese dinners invariably got from them a stronger, more visceral response than any others, even though I knew very little about cooking anything at all. Perhaps, I thought, people saw me as an authority because I ought to be; they couldn't see beyond my Chinese face to know that I had not grown up peeling fresh water chestnuts at my grandmother's side. They had a notion of my mother and me sitting before rows and rows of perfectly wrapped wonton, as the torch of Chinese home cooking was handed on, and preferred not to imagine that the kitchen of my childhood was just as likely to feature my brother and me heating up a frozen pizza just in time to watch a rerun of *Three's Company*. So, even after I became a competent cook, I tried not to hear praise for my Chinese cooking because I knew I was a fraud: In the same way that I had learned to speak Chinese in a classroom in college, I had learned to cook Chinese from books written in English, just like any other flatlander.

I don't know exactly how and when I realized that the novel I was writing was doomed. Maybe I was preparing a few chapters to send out, or maybe I was simply stepping back and taking an honest look at last. All I remember is that one day, after two or three hundred pages had piled up on the desk and my already-poor eyesight had further declined from staring at computer screens day and night, I saw that the whole thing, even with the moment of insight here and there and the reasonably competent writing, was a hoax—and not in the way that a good novel should be. My characters were facile constructs, made by an American writer projecting convenient, usually virtuous, personalities onto Chinese people. The cousin who teaches the American a thing or two about eating a balance of hot- and cold-element foods for health was just a device for transmitting what I had found interesting about Chinese medicine. The solemn grave-sweeping that takes place during Qing Ming actually takes place to open a narrative into recent family history, a history that I never actually heard any Chinese person relate. And the enormous sense of struggle and history that eventually gives the American character a sense of her identity as a Chinese American was totally fake, a carrot held out to the American consumer, who hungers for an identity, preferably exotic, that goes back farther than two hundred years.

I had to admit it before I dragged the effort out any longer. This was not the story that mattered to me. It was someone else's story, that of relatives I neither knew nor understood, and I did not have the personal stake in it that would make it ring true on the page. I had missed the point about the American character, whose real story was taking place back home, with jobs, parents, siblings, boyfriends, and friends. The Chinese stories I did possess were sketchy and delivered haphazardly in English by my mother, father, and other dear people in my life, such as my aunt from Savannah, who told me how the first silkworm eggs were smuggled out of China (in a woman's tall hairdo). "Facts" like this gave me a bit of authority in the schoolyard, but they hardly made me Chinese.

In fact, I was guilty of the very crime that others had committed every time they looked at me and saw a grandmother with bound feet or a Welsh corgi roasting on a spit. It was the offense one of my Atlanta neighbors had committed shortly after I returned from Shanghai, by suggesting that I study in England in order to experience a culture different from my own. In writing the novel, I had taken these misguided assumptions to heart and adopted, for the story's duration, a faux Chineseness that would allow me to tell the more exciting story, because it was too hard to find the revelatory aspects of my own, hopelessly peaceful, suburban life.

I do not remember this realization as devastating. It was, in fact, a relief. There had been so many compelling individual stories and such a preponderance of facts and characters that the undertaking had become impossible to control. I was glad to be free of the unwieldy, sprawling project. While poetry was not marketable like the Great Chinese American Novel, it had remained true for me, perhaps because of its lack of marketability, perhaps because of its (often misleading) lack of narrative. Each poem I wrote, whether it was about Apollo and Daphne or an empress or Tompkins Square Park or The People's Park, contained a kernel of personal truth. And a good poem, unlike my narrow-minded novel, could be read several ways, so that each reader could come away with something different.

I suppose I must have closed the notebook in which I had organized the pages of that moribund epic, sat back, and poked around the kitchen for something to eat. What about my Chinese cooking? I wondered. Is that fake, too? Am I just a Kraft Macaroni & Cheese kind of girl?

I had written the novel hastily, for fear of quitting, but I had taken the time to be accurate with food references: boiled meat dumplings for Beijing, soupy shrimp dumplings for Suzhou, fried oyster cakes for Xiamen, deep-fried carp and braised fava beans for Shanghai. I had consulted authoritative cookbooks as well as my parents and my China journals for proof of authenticity, and I had prepared many of the foods in the cookbooks for the fun of it. I had thought back to the gifts of "the snail-bun lady," the steamed fish and drunken chickens of various Aunties, the powerful bitterness of bitter melon, and the gleaming red strips of roast pork being basted in the oven. I even knew a little about chicken-slaughtering because my father had described it to us as one of his teenage chores when we complained about having to sweep the carport or wash the dog bowl.

The only thing that worked about my failed fiction was the food, and the reason was obvious. I was knowledgeable—and I cared— about Chinese food long before I ever set foot in Asia (or even learned the names for most of the dishes). My attachment to it was honest, cultivated at the dinner tables of childhood. Food had been the only aspect of daily life that truly set my family apart from our Southern neighbors, and thus food was the only thing that really made sense to me when I lived in China.

Perhaps, then, my Chinese dinner parties were not entirely fraudulent. Quite possibly, my Chinese culinary education had nothing to do with cookbooks, mine or my mother's, but with our eating of the stuff in America, whether in an Atlanta restaurant, the kitchen of an Auntie, or our own home; and similarly, my literary territory had far more to do with the elements of my own childhood than with the "heritage" I had tried to collect in language labs and on the road. My parents' sketchy anecdotes were more "authentic" than my superficial encounters with the actual people involved in the anecdotes. It was the force of narrative within my immediate family that mattered, not the hard facts. Some stories, like some recipes, are mine, and some belong to others. This is how I have learned to place a platter of Dongpo Rou before a gathering of hungry friends and to accept credit for understanding its spirit, but to keep my hands off the life-story of Su Dongpo, or anyone else, except those whose lives have honestly touched my own.

1998

She, without Apology

As a writer, I am sometimes plagued by voices in my head. Unfortunately, these are less often the voices of imagined characters than the voices of self-punishment.

"Adrienne," they hiss, "put down that cookbook *now*." "Get out of the kitchen or your poetry career is over." "Just make a huge pot of chili for the week and don't cook again until next weekend."

I talk back, which is why I mutter to myself in the supermarket: "If I stop reading cookbooks, I'll keep making the same things, and get bored with eating and bored with life." "There is no such thing as a poetry career." "Anything you eat seven nights in a row becomes something you don't want to see again for six months."

The voices of self-punishment always have fierce rebuttals, so I go through my days, which I spend whenever possible on things culinary and literary, feeling divided. Despite my affection for "culinary literature," I am not convinced that it is any less an oxymoron than "poetry career." Somehow, I long ago internalized the dim view that artists and intellectuals tend to take of cookbooks, which carry associations of harried mothers who, having dished up the same ground-beef casserole every week for twenty years, regret their lives.

At the same time, I am drawn to books about food. I care about food history, food-preparation techniques, nutrition, and agriculture, as well as the more obviously seductive panorama of world cuisines. I never got over my amazement at all of the things that can come from a lowly bag of flour: pasta, bagels, wonton wrappers, baguettes, mu shu pancakes, naan, tortillas, pretzels, breadsticks, dog biscuits, crackers, and pizza dough, for a start. Often, I feel compelled to make these things, as well as the sauces, spreads, fillings, and toppings that turn them into meals, rather than buying them, because I want to see proof that they all have their origins in the same crop, wheat. Sometimes, in the bookstore, I have no time for the poetry section despite the presence of my own book there; all life seems to reside in the cookbook section. And when I get a new cookbook, or re-enter the world of a dependable old one, I find myself wide awake at two in the morning, feverishly planning menus, and the next day I'm bullying the fish guy about freshness, just like the Chinese American matrons I swore in childhood never to become.

That is, I love to cook. And I still seek justifications for doing it so much. One excuse is that a good cookbook offers a reading experience not unlike that of a good collection of poems. Although there is a sense of progression from start to finish, the reader can also dip in anywhere and enjoy a fully realized, self-contained piece in a page or two. Certain pages invite rereading and copying for friends, and evoke different responses at different times in the reader's day, week, or life. Upon revisiting the book, the reader sees some things as if for the first time. (The dishes that popped out at me in general cookbooks changed after I took an interest in French cooking, and changed again after I studied Italian, and again after a brief trip to Germany. Similarly, the poems that jump out at me in any collection have changed each time my circumstances have, such as when I moved to New York, when I moved out of New York, when I got married, and after my grandparents died.)

Good cookbooks and good poetry collections, of course, are not static, but accommodate and inspire change as the reader changes. As a result, neither kind of book ever really ends. The plot cannot be spoiled. And both types of books, in their highest forms, are life-changing. For instance, just as the poems of Jane Kenyon induce me to write, think, and live with renewed honesty, so do the notes and recipes of Marcella Hazan inspire me to cook with greater purity, taking no shortcuts on ingredients or procedure. The results are palpable the same day.

Here is Jane Kenyon's brief poem "Biscuit":

> The dog has cleaned his bowl
> and his reward is a biscuit,
> which I put in his mouth
> like a priest offering the host.
>
> I can't bear that trusting face!
> He asks for bread, expects
> bread, and I in my power
> might have given him a stone.

I have seen people, at picnics, offer dogs stones. These people are not dog lovers, or they wouldn't do it. The narrator of "Biscuit" is tormented by the authority she wields over the dog, and by her power to have mercy or not have mercy. A person so tormented would not abuse that power, but implicit in the poem is the simple truth that bad dogs are created by bad people, or that our actions create reactions in the world. To behave with sensitivity and grace, to avoid doing damage, requires constant vigilance.

Marcella Hazan's introductory notes to *Essentials of Classic Italian Cooking* reflect a similar devotion to purity:

> Flavor, in Italian dishes, builds up from the bottom. It is not a cover, it is a base. In a pasta sauce, a *risotto*, a soup, a fricassee, a stew, or a dish of vegetables, a foundation of flavor supports, lifts, points up the principal ingredients. To grasp this architectural principle central to the

structure of much Italian cooking, and to become familiar
with the three key techniques that enable you to apply it,
is to take a long step toward mastering Italian taste. The
techniques are known as *battuto*, *soffritto*, and *insaporire*.

Hazan goes on to define *battuto* as the fine chopping of aromatics, such as onions, parsley, carrots, and celery; *soffritto* as the
carefully ordered sautéing of these ingredients in oil or fat; and
insaporire as the thoughtful combining of a dish's main ingredients
with the now-fragrant aromatics. Each step depends on the conscientious execution of the previous step, and all combine to bring out
the strengths of the central meat or vegetable, not to hide its weak-
nesses or to contrive a taste where there was none before. This is
honest cooking, the gently enhanced presentation of what nature
created.

Both writers go to the heart of the matter, the foundations of
action and consequences, and teach the reader to proceed honestly, with conscience, and with constant anticipation of both
short- and long-term results. Reading them, I pay better attention
to my dog in light of her total dependence on her humans, and I'm
more careful in the preparing of our own dinner—some of which
always becomes part of the dog's dinner, since, at the table, "I can't
bear that trusting face."

Despite all that it can teach me about purity, structure, or actions
and reactions in the world, and despite all the pleasure it brings,
cooking is sometimes the direct enemy of writing. Since I've entered
a field with slim financial rewards, I do not get to choose, from
night to night, between cooking and going out. I always have to
cook. And cooking well, even for someone who has a good kitchen
and the required skills, takes time. It requires frequent shopping,
good planning, and flexibility. It ropes you in, since meals are linked
by ingredients. That is, each cooking session leaves behind some

perishables, which you then have to think of tasty and practical ways to use in new dishes, which leave behind other ingredients, which lead to the next menu. All along, you feed new ingredients into the chain, maintaining freshness and novelty of taste—provided you have the energy and imagination to innovate—but also never being released from the cycle's day-to-day tyranny. Even a weekend out of town throws everything off, because something is invariably at a point where it will spoil in two days, and letting food spoil is a crime against which any thoughtful person's spirit rebels.

To escape this process, I have occasionally abandoned the kitchen and retreated to artists' colonies, where meals are provided. In a colony, I could spend the day reading and writing, taking breaks to roam the grounds or nap—giving not a thought to the planning of breakfast, lunch, or dinner—and a beautiful grilled chicken breast, rice pilaf, and steamed asparagus would magically appear on my plate at dinnertime. I could go a month without seeing the inside of a grocery store, eat well, write, and immerse my mind in the sort of books that draw respect in the worlds of art and academia, two worlds I was raised to respect.

Such retreats made me feel like the mythical artist whose household staff, or spouse and children, scurry around all day—doing the laundry, sweeping the floors, buying and cooking the meats and vegetables, then cleaning up afterwards—so that I might accomplish the lasting work. I wondered how I ever got anything done at home, not so much because of the actual distractions as because of the missing sense of importance. In the regular world, where you are the only person who treats your working hours as sacred, self-doubt becomes a fiercer foe than lack of time.

Colonies, however, also made me restless. I missed the tactile aspects of cooking, and grew envious of the visual artists around me, who worked with their hands, listened to music as they worked, and regularly went out into the world in search of materials—into the woods, to garbage dumps, to the grocery store. Trapped in stark silence, with little more than a supply of printer paper to maintain, I missed the physical rituals of lining up everything that was left in the fridge, imagining menus beginning with those things, and going out in search of the ingredients required to complete those menus—all tasks during which I did not aspire to brilliant literary thoughts. In a colony, even the reading of food history and cookbooks was not much fun without a kitchen and market in which to test out some of the ideas.

It was particularly hard to read about sourdough baking while knowing that my starter was at home, dying of starvation. So I put the food books aside and devoted the time to poetry, only to discover that reading (not to mention writing) poetry was not much fun without the parallel, daily experience of reading and employing cookbooks. My creative life was at its healthiest and most alive when I had both. I wasn't sure why. Was poetry for the mind (contemplation) and the cookbook for the body (action)? Was poetry art and the cookbook life?

These divisions did not seem fair. The best poetry gives the reader unambiguously physical sensations (as Emily Dickinson described them, feeling "so cold no fire can ever warm me" or "as if the top of my head were taken off"), and the best cooking gets an emotional as well as a physical response, sometimes because of the evocation of past people, times, or places, sometimes because of the simple genius in evidence. Great poetry is infused with the lived life, and nothing less than art goes into great cooking. The reason I needed to keep studying both, whatever it was, had little to do with the fundamental differences between poetry and cooking, for the more I learned about the two, the more similar they became.

Reading is a lifelong venture for anyone who cares about it, and becoming "well-read" is a process more dynamic than linear. One needs different books at different stages of one's life, and sometimes one needs the same books in different ways. For instance, many of the books that had a profound effect on me in high school—such as Ayn Rand's *The Fountainhead* and Sylvia Plath's *The Bell Jar*—would not strike me with the same force if I read them for the first time today. And conversely, I think that when I read *Macbeth*, *Dubliners*, and "The Love Song of J. Alfred Prufrock" in high school, I missed a great deal of what those works offer me now. I can't think of any dedicated readers who do not feel similarly about the books in their lives.

That is, reading in its most meaningful sense is anything but plowing through a list of great books. Plowing has its uses, such as earning a degree in English, but it invariably involves reading a lot of important books when you're not in the mood for them and putting off many equally important books that you are, at the moment, dying to read. Sometimes, by the time the latter come up on your list, you're not in the mood for *them*. You gain the desired knowledge at the desired time, but you don't necessarily do full justice to the books or yourself.

Nevertheless, plowing can give you a sense of order and progress, and make you feel that you are not reading haphazardly. Not having a degree in English myself, I sometimes decide to fill in some of the gaps on my own. I make reading lists, usually more ambitious than is practical. I tend to focus on the poetry of Britain, Ireland, and the United States but often include poets in translation, as well as novelists and essayists. I make an effort to include a range of time periods, so as not to get stuck, out of laziness, in the last century, which is of course the most accessible. There is usually a vague basis in other reading lists, mainly the canon as indicated in anthologies, textbooks, and the critical writings of authors and scholars, but also the odd review, friend's recommendation, or intriguing volume encountered in a bookstore. I make the lists on index cards, with just five or six authors, one to five works by each author, per card. Any more and I would be overwhelmed. I look at only one card at a time.

And here, examining the cards, I find the explanation: Invariably, my list contains mostly men. This is particularly obvious when it focuses on a time other than our own, but it holds even when it emphasizes modern times. Even taking into account the considerably larger number of women authors in the last century, it is only when I choose to emphasize women that my lists contain an equal proportion of women to men, and then it becomes a list with an emphasis on women authors, not just a list of authors.

This is not surprising. Nearly everywhere in the world, men have traditionally done the sort of creating that gets canonized, preserved in museums, and taught in schools (governing, philosophizing, waging wars, writing books), while women have done the sort of creating that does not get recorded (childbearing, child-rearing, housekeeping, gardening, cooking). This has been true even when men cook, for until very recently, men kept the arena of haute cuisine, the field of cooking in which a practitioner could achieve fame, to themselves, while women did the home-cooking, which at most got a little local, temporary recognition, and was generally taken for granted, like the laundry and sewing, by their families.

I suspect that I am driven to read cookbooks alongside literature because the two genres, read together, give me a long view of human creativity as achieved by both sexes, rather than by men plus a few exceptionally driven women.

There are many reasons why I think of cookbooks as feminine. Cookbooks are one of the few genres of writing in which female authorship has long been accepted; there has been little need to hide behind a male pen name, and the authors have not been denied an education, insofar as the home kitchen and garden have been the place of instruction. The first cookbook by an American was by a woman, Amelia Simmons (*American Cookery*, 1796); among its British predecessors distributed here were Hannah Glasse's *The Art of Cookery* (1747) and Hannah Woolley's *The Gen-*

tlewoman's Companion (1682). The most influential cookbook in American history was written by a woman; it was Mary Randolph's *The Virginia House-wife* (1824), which also happens to be the first American cookbook to have an essentially American, not English, identity. And the modern culinary pantheon of the English language includes such undisputed female stars as Julia Child, Alice Waters, M.F.K. Fisher, and Elizabeth David.

While cookbooks are generally seen as marginal to artistic accomplishment, I suspect that that's partially because they are often written by women, and partially because their concern—food—is seen as lowly by those intellectuals who would place nourishment of the mind above nourishment of the body. Such people have clearly not tried to think on an empty stomach, and I imagine that some of them are also so humorless and alienated from their bodies as to be indifferent to the way their food looks, smells, or tastes.

But perhaps most importantly to me—because a poet's first concern is language—cookbooks are the one print genre in which, reading historically, the impersonal third-person pronoun can very well be "she," without sounding like an intervention reacting to "he." In 2002, "he" still sounds the most natural, the enlightened alternatives almost always sounding like apologies: "He or she" disrupts a sentence, as does "she or he"; "s/he" is not pronounceable; alternating "he" and "she" in the same text sounds awful; "they" sounds plural; and "she" used alone is the original problem in reverse. And the ear is, finally, what determines usage.

In contrast, in a cookbook of any age, regardless of the sex of the author, you are perfectly likely to find a female mentor (perhaps even a servant or enslaved person, lending recognition to people more marginalized than women in general), feminine hands in explanatory sketches, paeans to a grandmother or mother's culinary genius (what would have become of James Beard without the education of his mother's cooking, not to mention the

Chinese chef, Let, who cooked in her hotel?), and the expectation of a female reader, which may well translate into the use of "she," without apology. The introduction to the 1931 *Joy of Cooking*, for instance, addresses a woman reader: "When you are entertaining, try not to feel that something unusual is expected of you as a hostess. It isn't. Just be yourself." (It goes on to refer to the guest as "he," but as women have long known concerning usage, you can't have everything.) In the foreword to *Mastering the Art of French Cooking* (1961), Julia Child and her co-authors take into account the circumstances of ordinary women's lives: "This book is for the servantless American cook who can be unconcerned on occasion with budgets, waistlines, time schedules, children's meals, the parent-chauffeur-den-mother syndrome, or anything else which might interfere with the enjoyment of producing something wonderful to eat." And in her celebrated *French Country Cooking* (1951), the British food revolutionary Elizabeth David places food preparation in the hands of women: "Rationing, the disappearance of servants, and the bad and expensive meals served in restaurants, have led Englishwomen to take a far greater interest in food than was formerly considered polite." In that sentence, men who cook at home are assumed to be included, just as women who do just about anything else have, for centuries, been assumed to be included under the pronoun "he" or the nouns "man" or "men."

Although the trend today is to use language that overtly includes everyone, plenty of earlier books that make no such effort have remained and will continue to remain central and relevant. Among them are the Bible and the writings of Confucius—texts so deeply at the heart of the civilizations they underlie that most people do not have to have read them to find themselves living by some of their teachings (although often the wrong ones—but that's another topic).

A few cookbooks whose language occasionally neglects to mention that men, too, can cook, seem a rather harmless blip in a tradition that, for most of its worldwide history, neglects to acknowledge that women, too, can read (never mind write, or exist). Consequently, when I'm working through one of my four-men-one-woman reading lists and starting to wonder what all those men's sisters would have accomplished if they had been allowed, I turn for a partial answer (and for dinner) to one of the volumes on the cookbook shelf and linger there a long time. I realize that the sisters are not all there, that most of the achievements of home cooks have been recorded without their names, that some such innovations were recorded against the inventor's will (a secret recipe being a key to power), and that many of those women, if born into today's world, wouldn't touch a frying pan with a ten-foot pole, but I am sure of one thing: Women through most of time are, by and large, silent in the field I've chosen—"literature"—and I'm hungry to know what they were saying, even if it was only how not to kill your sourdough starter, and even if their wisdom was put on paper posthumously, in the words of a son or nephew. As I learn the right touch for shaping a loaf of soda bread without toughening it, or smashing ginger and scallions to release their perfume but not their flesh, or evenly dressing a salad, I think I can almost see the deft hands of the women who in later times would have written novels, plays, music, or the law; I think I can feel their sharp eyes evaluating every last leaf at market, and hear the chopping, stirring, and sizzling of their artistry at work—sounds that begin, ever so slowly, to fill their tremendous silence.

2002

References

Child, Julia, with Louisette Bertholle and Simone Beck, *Mastering the Art of French Cooking,* volume 1 (New York: Alfred A. Knopf, 1961) vii.

David, Elizabeth. *French Country Cooking* (London: Penguin, 1951) 8.

Hazan, Marcella. *Essentials of Classic Italian Cooking* (New York: Alfred A. Knopf, 1992) 7.

Kenyon, Jane. "Biscuit" from *Otherwise: New and Selected Poems* (Saint Paul, MN: Graywolf Press, 1996) 187.

Rombauer, Irma S., and Marion Rombauer Becker. *Joy of Cooking* (New York: Signet, 1931, paperback edition) 9.

Terse Wisdom, Casual, Not Lofty:
Charles Wright at the University
of Virginia

To celebrate Charles, I quote here a few remarks of his—casual, not lofty—and describe how they have helped me live my life.

"How much were you making in New York and how much are you making here?"

I had dissolved a life in the city—job, apartment, literary community—to attend UVa, mainly because of its poetry trinity of Charles, Gregory Orr, and Rita Dove, but also because some part of me hoped to be able to live in the South. Born and raised in Atlanta, I'd long intuited that my home region did not embrace my membership, and New York had drawn me for the same reason it has always drawn certain people from the rest of the country—the sense of finally having found one's own tribe, in a crucible of creativity—but I wanted to see if I could go back to the South, even temporarily, on my own terms.

Now that I'd been in Charlottesville for a while, some of my friends in New York seemed threatened. They said, bluntly, that I had exchanged real life in the city for the unreal life of the university, that the true artist sticks it out in the world, that I was taking the easy way out. Their barbs struck at my own uncertainty, because some part of me did subscribe to the romance of moving to the city with a day job and a typewriter and eventually, through brilliance and pluck, transcending the realities of New York real estate and the likelihood of ever being paid for writing. That was how I'd ended up in New York in the first place.

Charles provided the best, briefest counterargument. My job, in educational publishing, had been no gold mine, but it had provided good benefits and the salary would have risen if I'd stayed. Now, in Charlottesville, out-of-state tuition having gobbled all but $36 of my fellowship, I still had to make a living, which I was doing by patching together freelance assignments from the editors I knew, never refusing anything, no matter how bad the timing or pay, and making do with less: cooking nearly every meal, wearing secondhand clothes, saving envelopes from bills as notepaper. A child of immigrants, I found that some of this came naturally, but as I washed and hung up Ziploc bags to dry, it became clear that this was certainly not the easy way out, nor was it what my parents, who'd sent me to Harvard, had envisioned for the next generation. As Charles so concisely made clear, I *was* sticking it out. "How much were you making in New York and how much are you making here?" he asked. His point? That money differences mattered, but what mattered more was that I was making *poetry* in Charlottesville. The true artist might be sitting in a bar on Avenue B, or at a seminar table in one of Thomas Jefferson's classrooms. Forms were just that: forms.

"WHEN PEOPLE MOVE TO CALIFORNIA, THEY DON'T COME BACK."

The poem up for workshop was mine, mercifully consigned to oblivion, though its subject has stuck: the complexities of women's liberation. Persuaded by professors that my generation of women would be defined by our achievements, not by whose wives or mothers we became, I was struggling with the impossibility of putting this ideal into practice.

I set the poem in the New York apartment of one such woman: single, smart, not her mother. Among the flaws in her outwardly successful life was that friends kept moving to California.

Charles got all the points about the real world's resistance to the just principle of feminism (gender equality!), but he focused on that California detail, probably because it was about life, while the rest of the poem was about an idea. "That part is devastating," he said, "because, when people move to California, they don't come back."

Coming from Charles, a poet whose California landscapes can be mentally moved into, this comment helped me name the knot of doubt from which I was writing—and will probably always be writing—and determine how to handle it.

"Why do all the young women wear those huge black boots?"

Charles asked me this more than once, mystified. Some of us—by no means all—wore Doc Martens. Unlike the shoes I might still be wearing if I'd never left Georgia, Docs did not squash your toes into points, exacting a lifetime of pain.

It mattered that Charles used the word *all*. Here I was, only six years post-escape, back in my native South, where all manner of footbinding (albeit psychological) was practiced on those who weren't born with the right characteristics, and already, *all* the young women were wearing huge black boots.

Only Charles could phrase such a question so that you felt included, rather than excluded, by your strangeness. Not only was a new world possible, but change could take root in how a thing was said.

"ONCE YOU START TEACHING, YOU CAN'T STOP."

Years after UVa, my first book out, I asked Charles for a recommendation for an academic job, despite not having taught since the program. My freelance writing—a better means of survival than scraping together part-time teaching slots—paid inconsistently. It did leave time for poetry, so I had the publications to qualify to teach full-time, but now I lacked classroom experience.

I also found it suspicious that a young writer could enter an MFA program, take workshops for two years, and emerge transformed from student to teacher. It seemed that one should put in more years of writing before calling oneself a professor of it. Thus, I'd been writing but was still a transient, while my college classmates bought themselves houses. I was living out of cardboard boxes in Provincetown, Massachusetts, where a small, impermanent community of writers and artists provided me a raw, creative energy in exchange for the practice of living frugally and doing without a house in summer.

But summer was annoyingly consistent—it turned up every year—and even winter in P-town was growing too costly for people like us to hang on.

"I don't know why I haven't tried harder to make myself a teacher," I said to Charles.

"It's good not to be in a hurry to start teaching," he replied, "because once you start, you can't stop."

Many years later, tenured, settled in the heartland, I get it. Teaching feeds writing but also robs it blind. Time has never again been abundant, and my writing community is strewn far and wide. Charles supported his students equally in our eagerness and non-eagerness to get on the tenure track, even if, in my case, it might not have been there later. I took Charles's injunction to mean *A literary life can be lived in many ways; the externals matter less than the essence.*

Twenty years after becoming his student, I see that, heeding Charles's remarks, I've mostly made the life I wanted, but thanks also to his terse wisdom, I made sure not to wait for any particular milestone—the last of the U-Hauls? another book? tenure? some prize? One could wait indefinitely—to start living it.

2011

What's in a Name

WHEN I GIVE my name out loud to a poet, often while having a book signed, I never have to spell my first name. I simply say, "Adrienne as in Adrienne Rich." Coincidence of first name is a small reason to feel connected to a prominent person, and Adrienne Rich provided me with plenty of better ones: poetry, feminism, motherhood, the quest for identity. And they were primary. But the name always mattered.

I discovered her work late in high school (unfortunately not *in* high school), in Hayden Carruth's anthology *The Voice That Is Great Within Us*. It was 1984, suburban Atlanta. Bookstore shelves asserted that "living writer" meant "male novelist": Updike, Mailer, Vonnegut. I read them hungrily but feared I was headed for "female poet," which clearly meant lifelong obscurity or, if one died young and spectacularly enough, tragic genius.

Adrienne Rich stood in contrast to that. Unlike almost every woman in my universe, she had both children and an artistic life, though not without great difficulty. She took on the same huge topics as the malest male novelist, but in non-sprawling literary forms. Her compact "Prospective Immigrants Please Note" told me that my parents had lived full lives before their arrival in this country:

> Either you will
> go through this door
> or you will not go through.

If you go through
there is always the risk
of remembering your name.

When they stayed up late in animated Chinese conversation with friends, my parents were half on the unseen other side of that door.

When I left for Rich's alma mater, its name had become "Harvard and Radcliffe Colleges." Male and female students had the same status, occupied the same buildings, and were viewed as going to Harvard, with all the history it implied. Those of us who aspired to lives of poetry looked back toward a daunting lot: Eliot, Frost, Stevens, cummings, Lowell, Ashbery. One had to look harder for the women—fewer, more recent, and identified with Radcliffe—but they were visionaries: Maxine Kumin, Jean Valentine, Adrienne Rich.

Most of my college years felt like Harvard, not Radcliffe, as I lived and went to class with the men, where men had lived and studied since 1636. But on occasion I went to Radcliffe Yard and wandered that less-trafficked area feeling awed, thinking almost aloud, Adrienne Rich climbed those steps. Adrienne Rich was once nineteen, too. A poet doesn't have to be named Thomas or Robert or John, or hide her gender with initials. A poet can be named Adrienne. Look around you; feel the earth beneath your feet. It happened right here.

2012

2

Everyone Has to Try

BETWEEN AND AMONG: NOTES
ON SECTION TWO

THE ESSAYS in this section are a mix of genres—personal reflections, craft lessons, the remembrance of a mentor—and a mix of lengths, but to my mind, they belong together.

That is, when I'm writing about craft, I'm constantly thinking about life, and when I'm writing about life, I'm constantly thinking about craft. This is my rationale for interspersing essays that may seem to belong to different literary families. They are meant not as a miscellany but as a journey of exploration, over time, of a range of preoccupations that turn out to be related.

As any good student of literature knows, form and content unfold in tandem; only in the coldest, most unpoetic calculation do they operate separately.

A note on "People Were Upset That People Were Upset": It has been seven years since I wrote the piece in 2016. The public debate over speech—how to be inclusive, how not to offend, who has the right to say what—has only intensified since. The essay reflects where I stood in 2016 on a controversy over a poem. As the discourse unfolded, I made an earnest effort to be honest and fair in my take on the controversy. Some of my circumstances have changed since that time: *The New Yorker* has published some of my poems; I no longer teach courses that involve critical papers; and my current students have spent a larger proportion of their lives in a fiercely divided political environment than my 2016 students had.

THE DOG COAT

I BROUGHT A dog-fur coat home from China in 1988, after an academic year there. Off-white, soft, and substantial, it was a gift from a great uncle I hadn't met until he came to Shanghai to greet me. He'd spent three days on a packed train to get there and had made the coat himself.

Although I recoiled from fur in stores, I'd never been confronted with the pelt of an animal with whom I might have shared daily life. Foxes, mink, and chinchillas were clearly worthy of consumer boycott, but this conviction had until now been more idea than feeling.

At the same time, I was being confronted with what I knew about my great uncle, whom my mother remembers as an animal lover and Chinese-opera fan. Unlike his brother, my grandfather, he didn't flee to Taiwan before the Communist takeover, although he was sure to pay for his landowning origins. We don't know why he didn't go, whether he even had the means.

Indeed, the family's houses in Shanghai were seized, my uncle exiled to the countryside. For four decades, he did physical labor in an impoverished southwestern outpost. He never married.

In the moment the coat was presented, it didn't occur to me to stage a one-student protest against dog fur. Instead, I thanked my uncle in my American-college Mandarin (which, no matter how well-pronounced, marked one as an outsider in Shanghai) and tried the coat on. What else was there to do? Although I couldn't banish the phrase "the dog coat" from my mind, I didn't find it repugnant, just disturbing. My uncle had next to nothing and wanted to give me something. Perhaps someone had used the flesh for food; the possibility somehow consoled me.

Some people will tell you, "The Chinese eat dogs," for shock effect, or to imply an inhumane, monolithic people. But my mother's family cherished their springer spaniel, Beauty, whom they had to leave in the care of household staff upon fleeing. Decades later, the mention of Beauty still moved my stoic grandparents.

Now, on the rare occasions when the coat comes up in conversation, I'm chilled by the righteous horror that sometimes follows. I struggle to create the context, to convey—as if it were a Chinese condition—that when a person loses everything overnight, for no reason, it's only natural to try to rebuild, using what resources happen to be available.

After leaving China, I stored the coat in my parents' house. I could neither wear it nor part with it. It stayed there until several years ago, when my parents moved into a retirement community and donated it, along with masses of other stuff, to Goodwill. Perhaps some unwitting person is wearing it now, oblivious to its origins, grateful to be warm.

2013

Where Are You Really From?
Reading and Writing Place
and Experience

Maxine Kumin's poem "Encounter in August" describes a standoff between gardener and black bear over a crop of beans:

> Inside the tepee that admits
> sunlight to the underpart
> he stands eating my Kentucky Wonders.
> Downs pod after pod, spilling the beans,
> the ones I'd saved for shelling out
> this winter, thinking *soup*
> when he'd gone deep, denned up.

The speaker stands ten feet from the bear and watches him devour her beans. The bear doesn't notice her while he polishes off the season's yield. The danger to the gardener goes unstated; mainly, we feel her indignation and loss. The encounter ends with the bear's oblivious departure and the speaker's effort to make peace with what has happened:

> At last he goes the way the skunk
> does, supreme egoist, ambling

into the woodlot on all fours
leaving my trellis flat and beanless
and yet I find the trade-off fair:
beans and more beans for this hour of bear.

For years I loved this poem, along with many others by Kumin; they fed my vision of her home in New Hampshire, Pobiz Farm, and the surrounding area. From "Taking the Lambs to Market," I imagined Amos the butcher; from "Nurture," I saw stray animals warming themselves by Kumin's fireplace; from "Woodchucks," I imagined Kumin struggling to protect her vegetable garden from devastation by woodchucks. In 2009, Kumin came to Dickinson College, where I teach, which gave me two precious days to talk with her about poems and life. "Encounter in August" was one of the poems I brought up.

"That one really happened," she said. "That was a real bear. It actually ate the beans from my garden."

Although I was pleased to know this, on some level I was disappointed—not in this poem, but in the fact of its being exceptional. If this one was notable for being true, then others were invented, or partially invented. Amos the butcher might be Jonas or Peter; it was possible that no one on Pobiz Farm had ever shot a single woodchuck. Even as I routinely urged students to alter facts for the sake of a poem's success, and did so myself, I had been unwittingly reading Kumin's poems as literal truth. Knowing that they might be fabrications did not diminish my regard for the poems, but discovering that I had somehow counted on their realness revealed that I had, over time, become attached to a person who was and was not the real Maxine Kumin.

This was as it should be, of course. "What really happened" is never the point. There's the life, and there's the work; the latter does not owe accuracy to the former. But still, I wanted the Maxine Kumin who was sitting next to me at dinner to be the Maxine Kumin who had lived in my readerly imagination for all of my writing life. My selfish desire to meet this fantasy person counted on her to exist as her words had led me to believe. (I'm sure there are parallels in online dating, but that's another essay.)

In the end, however, the disappointment was fleeting. Kumin's poems have such a close resemblance to Kumin's life that whatever is fabricated in them fits nicely into the larger picture of who she was. At Dickinson she spoke earnestly and with humor to a student audience about the situation depicted in her poem "Looking Back in My Eighty-First Year": reflections on her real-life decision, as a young woman, to turn down a fellowship to do literary studies in France, and instead settle down with the man she remained married to for the rest of her life. She talked with touching candor about her friendship with Anne Sexton, her beloved horses, her beloved dogs. Certain people and animals make it into her poems in the same spirit in which they existed in real life; whether or not the facts were exact, this was the kind of correspondence that made sense.

Robert Frost's "Birches," one of the first Frost poems I knew, evokes a rural landscape where snow and ice routinely weigh down branches. About the birches, the speaker observes:

> Often you must have seen them
> Loaded with ice a sunny winter morning
> After a rain. They click upon themselves
> As the breeze rises, and turn many-colored
> As the stir cracks and crazes their enamel.

Then he imagines a boy raised in that landscape expertly swinging on the branches:

I should prefer to have some boy bend them
As he went out and in to fetch the cows—
Some boy too far from town to learn baseball,
Whose only play was what he found himself,
Summer or winter, and could play alone.
One by one he subdued his father's trees
By riding them down over and over again
Until he took the stiffness out of them,
And not one but hung limp, not one was left
For him to conquer.

The poem goes on to describe the precision with which such a boy, uncorrupted by urban or even small-town entertainments, handles the branches, having taught himself in verdant solitude just how far up and out to climb without breaking them. Then the poet declares: "So was I once myself a swinger of birches. / And so I dream of going back to be."

This is only one of many Frost poems that mark him as a New England poet, but unlike many of the others, this one strongly implies that the speaker, like the boy he imagines, grew up there, ignorant of alternatives. Having no one to play with, he has always played with birches. He seems to be such a longtime native of this place that he hasn't thought to imagine what another childhood might have looked like. That the birches are "his father's trees" suggests, also, that his family has been here and nowhere else for generations.

Thus was I surprised in 2003 when, heading to Frost's house in Franconia, New Hampshire, now known as The Frost Place, for a summer as poet-in-residence, I began looking at Frost's life where previously I had looked only at the poems, and found out that he was from San Francisco. True, his relocation to New England had taken place when he was still a boy—age eleven—and his father had come from a New England family, but Frost had by no means grown up "too far from town to learn baseball." Frost's mother was from Scotland; his parents had met in Pennsylvania. Frost's native landscape hadn't seen much in the way of the snow and ice-storms in "Birches." If he had in fact acquired such excellent birch-bending skills, it would have been in early adolescence, with full awareness that he wasn't in San Francisco anymore.

I was surprised, but not betrayed—not even annoyed. Learning this felt similar to the little surprises that arise in the study of food: corned beef and cabbage do not constitute a normal meal in Ireland; tomatoes aren't native to Italy; no one eats General Tso's Chicken in China (except now, on occasion, as an American import). Our notions of authenticity are often manufactured by marketing people, or based on some arbitrarily timed snapshot of what happens to inhabit a particular culture at a particular moment. Why should a poet's identity be any different, given that a poet, like a restaurant or tourism board, is packaging an identity through a body of work?

A child of immigrants, I took heart in seeing Frost as a kind of immigrant to New England. It meant—his father's family notwithstanding—that a person from elsewhere could become a local there, in the public sense if not in the neighborhood. And surely his having come from somewhere else gave him the perspective it would take to portray New England in such credible, memorable detail. The boy who's been swinging from birch branches all his life doesn't know what's extraordinary about it because he's never known a life in which he didn't swing from birch branches. Thus the outsider poet creates the sense of place and, by being widely read, the place itself. Again, the self created by the poems doesn't have to match the self who lived the life, although, as with Kumin, the multitude of resemblances enhance verisimilitude. Kumin herself is often compared to Frost as a portrayer of New England life, lived close to the earth. And lest we forget, Maxine Kumin came from Pennsylvania.

Several years ago, the poet Nick Carbó, guest-editing an Asian American issue of the online journal *MiPOesias,* asked me and a number of other Asian American poets for poems on the theme "I Will Not Love You Long Time." I had nothing lying around that fit the theme, so I figured I'd better write something. In any case, I found the prompt irresistible. It evoked for me the many family members—mostly older—whose English was that of a non-native speaker, but whose phrasing in English sometimes made for more effective statements than the grammatically correct version would. I'm convinced that, just as Frost and Kumin's non-New-England beginnings surely sharpened their perceptions of New England, my relatives' non-English-speaking beginnings gave me an under-standing of English that I would not have had if I'd grown up entirely among native speakers of it. Hearing things said in non-standard ways illuminated the standard ways and suggested that there were alternatives to "correct" language. I liked, also, the idea that anyone who says, "I will not love you long time" is simultane-ously admitting love for the addressee and declaring the imminent end of that love. It's a breakup statement at once decisive and vul-nerable. Its grammatical awkwardness adds a layer of difference, conveying that the "I" and "you" come from different cultural back-grounds, and that both their love and their estrangement tran-scend these differences. Another thing that remains unknown is who left whom: the "I" might be reacting to having been left, or the "I" might have made a decision to leave, despite residual feelings of attachment.

I had no idea that the line was a reference to a scene from *Full Metal Jacket,* in which a Vietnamese prostitute approaches two white American GIs with various lines in broken English, among them "Me love you long time," nor did I know that "I will not love you long time" had become a slogan among Asian Americans fed up with sexual stereotypes of Asian women. But all of that worked out fine with the poem I ended up writing, "Sestina," in which the speaker addresses a man who has said whatever he needed to say to get her to sleep with him, after which he runs for the hills. I relished playing with the language, which is how the poem became a sestina, its repetitions intended to reflect the human tendency to justify decisions we may know to be poor. I gave the speaker a Chinese grandmother who, like my own grandmother, lived in Communist China throughout the speaker's life and died before the speaker, an American, could visit or even emerge from childhood. The speaker mentally consults the grandmother for advice throughout the brief relationship, but of course the speaker has to invent the grandmother and provide the grandmother's replies herself, in deliberately broken English. As the speaker tries to navigate the emotional fallout, she finally admits that the grandmother is a fiction and she is on her own:

> The real grandmother—
> who knows what she would have wanted?
> Maybe she would've said, *This time*
> *different; for this man, first-sight love;*
> maybe she abhorred the limits of ancient wisdom
> on female joy. So I took you at your word.
>
> Now I'm putting words in my grandmother's
> mouth again, vessels for wisdom that's wanting:
> *Tell bad man, I will not love you long time.*

I think of the poem as depicting a commonplace experience—who hasn't misjudged a relationship or cast about for what an unavailable confidante would have said?—and not anything in particular about my own life. I don't think of my own life as interesting enough to be of consequence on the page, except insofar as episodes that *seem* to come from my life can shed light on someone else's life. And on one level, I cringe to think that someone reading the poem might take this to be an actual recounting of an experience, because it's fiction and I want it to be understood that way, except that it also isn't, because it's true to what I know and understand about negotiations between the sexes in a "liberated" society, both generally between women and men but also particularly between Asian women and white men—as well as between Asian American women and traditional Asian attitudes toward women, in this case represented by an imagined grandmother.

On another level, though, I think I've accomplished what I set out to accomplish when a reader thinks it's real. It means I've created a credible speaker and situation, and persuaded someone to believe in the integrity of the story. Some poems, like "Encounter in August" and "Birches," invite the reader to believe that the poet is the speaker, and as reader I've taken them up on it and derived more pleasure from the poems thanks to that credence. My effort in "Sestina" makes a similar invitation, much as I'd prefer not to seem like this speaker. If this means that I have to go around seeming to have been an idiot at least once, so be it: I'm not writing in order to seem virtuous or wise, but to be believed.

2014

PEOPLE WERE UPSET THAT
PEOPLE WERE UPSET

"IN THE PAST, death was often a source of suffering." "The poem is universal because it involves a birth and all readers have experienced being born."

Those are fictional examples, but anyone who grades papers will recognize the awkward effort to please a poorly imagined reader. Paralyzed by fear of being wrong, smart students at times produce absurd, robotic-sounding statements. Their teachers, convinced we've failed, laugh so that we won't cry.

That's why, when teaching literature, I sometimes encourage writing non-analytically. My specialty is poetry writing, so it's partially an invitation to creative writing. In my intro-level class "Literature and Food," students can write, in lieu of one critical paper, a personal essay that aspires to a distinctive voice and narrative arc, in the tradition of Laurie Colwin or M.F.K. Fisher.

Most take this option. Stiffness vanishes; personality emerges. No longer afraid of being wrong, students do what good writers have always done, muck around in gray areas. The best question themselves: disdaining their parents' taste; going abroad fearing the food; going next door fearing the food. Sometimes these pieces make me want to cry, too, but for the right reasons. They tell engaging stories that examine the pain and contradictions of everyday life.

Yet writing creatively also hazards being wrong, possibly more egregiously. Writers can be humanly, versus analytically, wrong. My most ambitious students risk sounding judgmental of less sophisticated eaters (classist), ungrateful to their parents (privileged), or like American tourists sampling "the curry" (racist, imperialist). In workshop sessions, which help the writer discover whether the intent of the piece has been realized, the class critiques everything, so it's not just between the author and me: the author's reputation is at stake.

They leap anyway. Even in dangerous territory, before they have command of form, my students are capable of being inquiring, genuine, and self-aware, because they rarely use constructions that fail to consider a wide range of possible readers. Having grown up hearing national discussion of gay marriage, racial injustice, unequal pay, transgender rights, weight discrimination, access for people with disabilities, treatment of undocumented immigrants, and religious intolerance, they navigate the possibility that their readers may include people in the affected groups with relative ease.

Sure, they trip up, as do I. (Growing older while they do not, I rely to a degree on conversation with them to keep me fluent in our constantly renewing language.) And our campus climate, like most colleges', still needs work; outside class, some still say terrible things.

Inclusivity efforts can also backfire. After the student protest at Oberlin College over cultural appropriation of foods, I briefly froze while planning a dinner in honor of a visiting writer. Our campus dining services, whose catering menu offers mainly American dishes of European origin, had always been helpful. To branch out, I could ask them to go off-menu and cook something non-Western. But if it didn't go as imagined, would people take offense? I didn't dare.

This month, when I saw Calvin Trillin's *New Yorker* poem, "Have They Run Out of Provinces Yet?", I wanted it to be harmless.

I tried to read its "we" (food-obsessed Americans being mocked) and "they" (bringers of Chinese food to the U.S. over decades) as ironic, and to take its goofiness as a sign that the wink was coming. But after multiple readings, "they" still remained foreign. At no point does the "we" allow for Chinese ancestry, although Chinese immigrants obviously run the restaurants all along. They and their descendants never become American.

No big deal, I told myself. You're just rattled because you happen to be a Chinese American poet who's into food and has a food-literature pantheon that includes Trillin; you happen to be working on a book of poems about American Chinese food over the last half-century, and incidentally just submitted some of those poems, in a fit of wild hope, to *The New Yorker.* You're the one person this poem wasn't meant for. It's unlucky, not malicious. If *The New Yorker* cared enough to aim this poem specifically at you, you'd have a much lighter teaching load.

But I couldn't sleep. The problem went beyond me, beyond Chinese Americans. The progress of language was being undone. Racially exclusive usage was thriving, not just in Trump brochures, but in our most prominent literary platform. Seeing the Asian American Writers' Workshop's call for responses, I wrote a poem that gives my take on what Trillin calls the "Simple days of chow mein and no stress." It arrived in a few fevered hours, quickly announcing itself as a villanelle, a form I learned not from Li Bai or my namesake Su Dongpo, but from Dylan Thomas and Elizabeth Bishop.

The outcry that greeted Trillin's poem affirmed that I was not the only person troubled by it. I first heard it from Asian Americans, but also from whites and other people of color.

Then came the backlash, mostly but not exclusively from whites, and disappointingly, from some white liberals: People of color need to "lighten up." So now a white person can't write about Chinese food? Give me a break.

It wasn't the first time members of the dominant group were telling a minoritized group how to feel. But I had underestimated the degree to which our nation is divided. I was hearing dismissive contempt from people I thought would have my back, even professors and poets, who know that "it's just a poem" doesn't hold up.

Their frustration, I gather, comes from feeling oppressed by the increasing number of ways they could get into trouble. Speech keeps becoming more fraught with the fear of being humanly wrong.

Anyone can write about Chinese food. It's a matter of usage, and usage *is* more complex than it was a generation ago. Because our population is always changing, because we keep acknowledging more groups that were always there, American writers must continually re-imagine our audience. Our youngest writers know the new rules best.

There's always conflict as language adapts. I only wish the discussion, like the discussion of who should lead the nation, were not so hatefully splintering us. Contempt is born of fear, and fear makes us say ridiculous things.

2016

The Way to the Heart Is Through the Ear

POETS OFTEN remark that being happy, especially in romantic love, results in stretches of not writing, or stretches of writing poorly. Lacking Frost's "lump in the throat," they don't have much to say because they're too busy living their bliss. This is not to say that there aren't reams of enduring love poems, suitable for weddings and the best love letters, but most poets write better when disturbed or conflicted, even about something far away in time or space. And most people who read poetry outside the classroom are seeking comfort or understanding from it because, in the moment, those things aren't available elsewhere.

Two of my favorite contemporary love poems, "So What If I Am in Love" by Molly Peacock and "Looking Back in My Eighty-First Year" by Maxine Kumin, manage to have it both ways. Both celebrate romantic love without giving the reader that queasy sensation of scrolling through a social-media feed in which everyone else is living a happier and more beautiful life. This essay explores how these two poems succeed, then offers a prompt for writing a poem in similar territory.

Peacock, known for adeptness with meter and rhyme, uses irregularly rhymed tercets to describe a New York City subway ride in the immediate aftermath of a night that must be kept under wraps if the speaker wants her life to proceed without crisis. Her new lover has lent her an old sweatshirt to sleep in, then given it to her to keep:

> The penguin sweatshirt I slept in smelled both
> of him and time, if time has odor, worn,
> softened as skin asleep, blurred as the breath
>
> beneath the faded lines of a bird born
> on a shirt, not in a nest. Completely torn
> between delight and the imagined wrath,
>
> the sheer disaster of my life torn down if
> the shirt were ever found, I accepted...

This economical opening not only lays out the situation clearly but also provides plenty for the ear: the off-rhymes of "both," "breath," "wrath," "if," and "with" operating against the exact rhymes of "worn," "born," and "torn," which also converse with the interior rhyme of "my life torn down." Meanwhile, "blurred" is echoed in "bird," "delight" in "life," "breath" in "nest." The penguin on the shirt is wearing off—"the faded lines of a bird"—but through its scent and softness, a new passion is being "born." The "delight" the speaker feels is tempered by "the imagined wrath, / the sheer disaster of my life torn down / if the shirt were ever found"; she tries to quash her elation and fit herself back into the life she was living before this encounter. Yet:

> ...I accepted
> his gift and got on the subway with
>
> my makeup, my papers, my underwear
> all stuffed in the bag where it lay, given,
> given to me! in my lap in the glare

of trainlight. "Beware," the panic-driven
self says, "No, you can't," even
at the cost of your growth. But I left it there.

With the rhymes of "underwear," "glare," and "there," interspersed
with "given" (which occurs twice), "driven," and "even," the word
"accepted" in the third stanza now sticks out as the only unrhymed
end word in the first five stanzas. "Accepted" is the wild card, the
speaker's incipient willingness to violate both her rhyme scheme
and her life. By taking the incriminating gift of the sweatshirt, she
has signed on to the new relationship—or she thinks she has. And
then there's a turning back: "But I left it there."

    The poem doesn't specify whether she leaves the bag on purpose
or by accident; presumably it's both, a mixture that expresses her
ambivalence: it would be so much more convenient not to love
this person, "even / at the cost of your growth." Can't she walk away
from him, just as she can walk away from the sweatshirt? As soon
as she jumps out onto the platform without the bag, she looks back:

> When the doors opened, I leapt out, turned around,
> saw it on the seat as the train rushed past,
> screaming "No!" so loud a man turned around.

There is no need to describe the setting; we gather from this brief
interaction that the station is crowded, the trains mercilessly effi-
cient, the bag irretrievable. That "a man turned around" evokes
the human activity around her and—except for that one man—its
indifference to her loss. Soon the man, too, is gone, into the bowels
of a city that runs on "cash":

> "I left a gift on the train," I said, aghast.
> "At least it wasn't cash," he said while the past,
> worn, softened, blurred as the lines of the bird,

a comic little figure in the arctic waste
of the white shirt, unfroze inside me, stirred
by the loss and relieved by what I dared

at last to feel.

When the rhyme of "past," "aghast," and another sense of "past"—
playfully intertwined with "cash"—turns into the off-rhyme of
"waste," we see that this moment is going to lay waste to her existing relationship, to her familiar life. She is "aghast" but has no
choice. What is represented by the "bird" has "stirred" elemental
feelings; seeing it carried away into the subway system's hundreds
of miles of track has clarified her wishes.

I have no idea what Peacock's drafts look like, but from my own
longtime experience with rhyme, I imagine that searching for
rhymes gave rise to "arctic waste," which, combined with the penguin, paved the way to the imagery of the closing lines:

> ...I wobbled home as if
> tossed from floe to floe of a broken jam,
> from if, to am, to so what if I am.

The image of a person "tossed" from one ice floe to another perfectly sets up the three-part last line, which is as much about language as it is about emotion. "So what if I am" combines "what if
I'm in love?" and "I am in love" with the surface recklessness of a
decision that isn't reckless at all. The apparent shrug of the title—
"So What If I Am in Love"—has turned out not to be a shrug at all,
but the culmination of an agonizing struggle.

The poem contains as much harmony (rhyme) as it does conflict
("the panic-driven / self" versus "delight"). The ending is anything
but glib; the speaker has been buffeted by forces larger than herself, which are not only the circumstances of her life but also the

ancient conventions of poetry: rhyme and orderly stanzas. These forces make her decision, like the lines of her poem, less negotiable and not entirely in her hands. To me this poem is both a musical pleasure and compelling evidence that love succeeds—and fails—for reasons that are often beyond an individual person's control. There is room in this poem not only for the lucky, but also for the unlucky, in love.

Maxine Kumin's "Looking Back in My Eighty-First Year" depicts the beginning of what, in the poet's life, turned out to be a long, happy marriage. It opens with an epigraph from Hilma Wolitzer that addresses the shock of aging: "How did we get to be old ladies—my grandmother's job—when we were the long-leggèd girls?"

Rare is the young bride who doesn't have some anxieties about her decision; exacerbating this speaker's doubt is the specific opportunity she has turned down to get married:

Instead of marrying the day after graduation,
in spite of freezing on my father's arm as
here comes the bride struck up,
saying, I'm not sure I want to do this,

I should have taken that fellowship
to the University of Grenoble to examine
the original manuscript
of Stendhal's *Lucien Leuwen*,

Immediately we discern that this young woman is an intellectual, her graduation a college one, most likely with high honors. Looking at the poet's dates, 1925-2014, this wedding is probably taking place in the mid-1940s. How many brilliant women of that time had potential careers shut down right after graduation with the striking up of "Here Comes the Bride"? Although this poem is here to show us that things went otherwise for this woman, we feel the loss of the many others who could have done scholarly work on Stendhal but instead disappeared into domestic duty.

It's also a fraught time to go to Europe:

> I, who had never been west of the Mississippi,
> should have crossed the ocean
> in third class on the Cunard White Star,
> the war just over, the Second World War
>
> when Kilroy was here, that innocent graffito,
> two eyes and a nose draped over
> a fence line. How could I go?

At first glance, "How could I go?" seems to refer to the speaker's lack of experience. It would be dangerous to take this journey in the immediate aftermath of the war, but especially perilous for a book-ish young woman "who had never been west of the Mississippi." Then we get the next line—"Passion had locked us together"—and the question becomes less about safety and more about her attach-ment to the beloved. She can't go because she's in love.

And yet it is only human to wonder, all these decades later, whether she could have had both the marriage *and* the fellowship. This is the germ of the poem, its conflict, the slight edge that reveals that everything isn't perfect.

This is also when the poem starts to rhyme in earnest. In the first three stanzas, one has to search for the rhymes, and it would be reasonable to argue that those stanzas don't rhyme. An enthu-siast for off-rhyme, I'm tempted to pair "arm as" with "do this," as well as "struck up," "fellowship," and "manuscript," but I'm not sure many would agree, and indeed the relatively prose-like rhythm discourages us from hearing them as rhymes. I would also connect "examine," "Leuwen," and "ocean," and while these are a bit easier to defend, they are not as audible as most of Kumin's rhyming in other poems, and the ear isn't primed to hear them, thanks to a preponderance of unrhymed end-words and the visual but not aural rhyme of "White Star" and "Second World War." Yet these hints of rhyme, however remote, are important because they make it possible for the poem to launch into full rhyme later.

By stanza four, we encounter not only "over" and "together" but then: "Sixty years my lover." The rhyme holds as we jump forward through time to Kumin's eighty-first year:

> Sixty years my lover,
> he says he would have waited.
> He says he would have sat
> where the steamship docked
>
> till the last of the pursers
> decamped, and I rushed back
> littering the runway with carbon paper...
> Why didn't I go? It was fated.

Now we have not only "over," "together," and "lover," but also "locked" echoed in "docked," the less-conspicuous "sat" and "back," and the more forceful "waited" and "fated." (I'd rather not get into any fights about whether "pursers" and "paper" rhyme.) The path the young bride didn't take—going to the University of Grenoble—is mostly unrhymed. The life she did live, on the other hand, is cemented, also, by a more iambic rhythm. Rhyme and meter, as they often do, make these stanzas—and thus this outcome—feel inevitable, "fated."

The final stanza could only have been written in old age:

Marriage dizzied us. Hand over hand,
flesh against flesh for the final haul,
we tugged our lifeline through limestone and sand,
lover and long-leggèd girl.

The two short declarative sentences—"It was fated" and "Marriage dizzied us"—would not work without the surrounding imagery and rhyme. The image of an older couple "tugg[ing] our lifeline through limestone and sand" and of a young couple reuniting at a dock, the ever-literary woman "littering the runway with carbon paper," create them as knowable characters. The powerful "lover and long-leggèd girl" bring back the smitten young couple who have now been married sixty years. The tight rhyme of "hand" and "sand" as well as the slight off-rhyme of "haul" and "girl" seal the poem, just as that early decision, requiring sacrifice on her part, sealed a meaningful promise. Still, the heart of the poem is doubt. It is not a poem of regret, but there is a layer of wistfulness, of normal human wondering.

"Looking Back in my Eighty-First Year," in all its strength, could also function as an occasional poem (and perhaps it has), read aloud to friends and family at a sixtieth-anniversary party. Picture dinner guests following along on the back of a menu card: Kumin's graduated rhymes answer the ear's need for song while also providing loose organizing principles for her quatrains, which visually mete out the years and facilitate transitions in thought, feeling, and time. Meanwhile, Peacock's "So What If I Am in Love," taking place in a smaller timespan, uses more frequent and audible rhymes that, too, organize the tercets, justify enjambments, convey crucial information without sounding explanatory, and entertain by both shape and sound. Once, these formal elements were the definition of poetry. Now that writing in rhyme and meter is anything but the default, poets must consciously decide when to do so. It might pay off especially well in love poems, where conflict is in shorter supply than in unhappier poems. Formal elements themselves can act as sources of tension, even suspense. The reader, along with the poet, wonders what is going to rhyme with "down if," or "examine." A stanzaic pattern, once established, can be adhered to or disrupted, to convey conformity, transgression, or transgression within conformity; a moment of hesitation ("I'm not sure I want to do this") can be brushed aside because it has brought us to the end of the quatrain, so it's time to walk down the aisle of white space; elation can be dramatized by repetition within the constraints of short lines: "given, / given to me!" There are simply more walls to gentle-collide with in a formal poem, and some topics need more collisions than others.

In 2009—her eighty-fourth year—I had the good fortune to invite Maxine Kumin to Dickinson College for a two-day residency. She read this poem, among others, to an appreciative audience, and during the Q&A, a student asked her, "What do you think would have happened if you'd gone to Grenoble?"

Kumin's reply made us all laugh: "I probably would have fallen in love with a Frenchman and run away."

We loved her for that and much more about the visit; the same honesty gives the poem its vitality. We also knew that Victor Kumin supported her passion for poetry; a husband who did not do so, with three children born in the ensuing years, might well have ended his wife's career as a poet before it began. The life-altering choices most people make in their twenties have long, unforeseeable effects. To consider this, from any point in life, is dizzying.

PROMPT: Consider a marriage or other romantic partnership that you think you don't quite understand. It doesn't have to be your own; it could be your parents' or grandparents', or that of a friend or other relative, or of public or fictional figures. In fact, it may be easiest to write about a relationship you don't know that much about, because you will be free to imagine much of it. Look for a pivotal moment in that relationship—if not the beginning or end, then maybe a period of doubt when, for instance, one emigrated with the promise to bring the other later, or when a struggle between them began, whatever the outcome. Consider rhyme and received form as receptacles that might help you organize the material and bring in unexpected images. Give the formal elements room to be irregular, and to make their needs known later in the process, certainly not in the first draft or two.

2018

WEDDING GIFTS
Adrienne Su

Everywhere, a reason for caution:
crystal bowls, white teacups, porcelain.

Objects, which used to tumble in
on their way to the junk heap,
now possessed origins.

I had no idea what to do with a dog
that didn't come from the pound,

and now, as if suddenly old,
found frailties in places I never knew existed.
Casseroles leapt, glasses imploded—

I wept each time. I knew from poetry
that no one conquers entropy,

but I also knew from poetry
everyone has to try. Rescued, the animal
loses all anonymity

in a syllable, and the hero's nobility
dissolves into family.

Marriage is the same, with dishes and rings.
Vows or no vows, you embrace your own death,
journeying to which, you only get clumsier, and things,

which you thought mere material,
become irreplaceable.

THE RISKY, THE BOLD, THE AUDACIOUS:
A REMEMBRANCE OF LUCIE BROCK-BROIDO,
1956-2018

THE LAST TIME I saw Lucie Brock-Broido, we were shopping at my local Target, in Carlisle, Pennsylvania, in 2006. The previous night, she had given a fierce, and fiercely funny, reading at Dickinson College at my invitation, and now she was about to drive back to New York. In addition to the reading, a class visit, and a party at my house, Lucie had agreed to an informal gathering with students, on the condition that it take place in a Starbucks.

Carlisle's only Starbucks is inside Target. My memory of that session is mainly of the late-afternoon sun making it difficult to see anyone, and of exhaustion from having stayed up most of the night after the party talking with Lucie, whose nocturnal ways seemed both cause and effect of the otherworldliness of her poems.

No one but Lucie Brock-Broido had ever been allowed to smoke in my house; my tiny kitchen made it smokier. "I'm going to be fifty!" she had said over the "wonton soup without wontons" that she had requested. "Isn't that an unbelievable injustice?" And I was going to be forty. It didn't seem possible that just over a decade separated us. As my professor in college, she had appeared as wise and formed as I was unwise and unformed.

Now, the students having gone back to campus, Lucie and I walked out of the Starbucks and into the Target. One of the worst things about New York City, we agreed, was that you couldn't bring home carloads of cleaning products, shampoo, and toothpaste from megastores. She piled her cart with daily things—most memorably, huge packs of paper towels and toilet paper. For me, for reasons I can't remember, she threw in a multipack of Pringles. At the checkout, she joked to the cashier that I was the one buying the toilet paper, and wasn't her friend going overboard? We piled everything into her car, I told her how to get on I-81 and thanked her for the visit and the Pringles, we hugged, and she drove away.

I met Lucie in the fall of 1988, my last year at Harvard. I had spent the previous year at Fudan University in Shanghai, where I hoped to find a world of poetry more or less like the contemporary American one, but in Chinese. That was, of course, one of the many ways in which I was unwise; I did not appreciate how unfree Chinese speech was and how little space its population had for literary anything. Another unwise motivation was that I had convinced myself that the English literary canon didn't want me and I needed to connect with the Chinese one. Of course, true to everyone's warnings, the People's Republic of China in 1987–88 turned out to be an oppressed and oppressive place, bearing little resemblance to the China I had constructed in my head from the Penguin *Poems of the Late T'ang*, the *Analects* of Confucius, the folktales from my language classes, and my parents' pre-Communist childhood anecdotes.

So by the time I met Lucie at a reception after a literary event at Harvard, I finally knew the obvious, that English was in every way my mother tongue and I was to some degree in the wrong major: East Asian Languages and Civilizations. It wasn't fully wrong; I had simply come to understand that I had chosen it out of love for the study of languages, the point of which was to give more dimension to my use of English. I cherished my East Asian coursework, classmates, and professors, and had come back from China only to throw myself into the study of Japanese, which was completely unnecessary from a course-credit point of view but which deepened my understanding of syllabic verse forms, sentence fragments as a literary device, gendered speech, and a range of grammars (loose in Chinese, strict in Japanese, and strict with a thousand irrational exceptions in English). My proposed senior-thesis topics kept getting rejected because they were Asian American rather than Asian, and creative rather than scholarly. If they belonged anywhere, it would be the English department, for which it was much too late.

Lucie's first question, "What are you doing?", allowed me to sum everything up. I explained that all I wanted to do was write poems. Would it be all right if I just didn't write a thesis? It would make me ineligible for honors beyond *cum laude*, and that was a bit of a drag because I'd been doing well, but would it ever matter?

She urged me to take her workshop, which was, like many things at Harvard, by application only. And then she spoke to me as if I were an actual poet: "If you write ten good poems in the next year, it'll mean a lot more to you than a thesis."

Now a seasoned professor myself, I ask: Who says this to an undergraduate, especially one whose poems you have never seen?

Lucie was the person I needed to meet at that juncture, an unusual teacher willing to do the reckless thing on behalf of poetry: to bet on the student's ability, rather than her likely inability paired with grandiosity. She herself had done something far more drastic, and much earlier in life, in service to poetry. As she told *Guernica* magazine in 2013,

> I came to poetry because I felt I couldn't live properly in the real world. I was thirteen and in Algebra class. That was the day I decided I would be a poet for all time. I walked out of class and dropped out of school. That doesn't mean I became a poet, but I did have this abso-

lute severance with one period of my life where I felt I
was being made to live in the world I was brought into—
Straight-A student, The Most Perfect Little Girl—that I
couldn't inhabit anymore.

The specifics are a bit more complicated; Lucie did not technically
drop out, but she seems to have made a decision to stop trying to
please every teacher and administrator, eventually switching to
an alternative school where she could work independently. It was
probably not obvious then that she would one day be a celebrated
professor at Harvard and Columbia. By Lucie's standard, I was
coming to my "dropping-out" awfully late, and it was not much of
one, especially when you looked to certain famous Harvard examples—Frost and Stevens, for example, didn't even get their degrees.

As it turned out, three of the poems I wrote in her class made
it into my first book, *Middle Kingdom*, which appeared eight years
later, in 1997. Three poems may not sound like a lot, but all working poets know how many poems get thrown away, or at least filed
in an archive of failures, on the way to a finished manuscript. One
of the three was later revised again, but the kernel of its origin—a
prompt from Lucie to write a "self-portrait"—remained the same.
Another generous poet-guide, Mark Doty, whom I met in Provincetown, convinced me years later to make that poem, "Address," the
opening poem to the book.

Now that I have published my fifth book, I can look back at the
first poem in my first book and think of it as exactly what Mark
called it—an announcement, a declaration of who I was going to
be. I was going to write about what it means to be American, in all
its confusion concerning race, language, class, and lore. I have not
always written specifically about that, but over twenty years later, it
is exactly what I'm doing.

I have saved Lucie's comments:

Adrienne Su
3/9/89
Self-Portrait

Address

"a native agent" *"buyer"*

There are many ways of saying Chinese
in American. One means restaurant.
Others mean comprador, coolie, green army.

I've been practicing
how to walk and talk _____ ? *lovely*
how to dress, what to do in a silk shop.

less effective if it all repeats?

How to talk. America: Meiguo,
second tone and third.
The beautiful country. *chills down the reader's spine !!*

In second grade we watched films
on King in Atlanta
and the ships at Old Gold Mountain.
They said we had hidden the Japanese
in California.
Everyone apologized to me.

why choose to break the form here? (3 elsewhere) why not continue in the surge of tercets.

If I'd known, I might have explained.
Anything would have been credible:
Chinese, Thai, Filipino.

I'm lost?

I am from Eldorado Drive
in the suburbs. In the mirror
I see aberrations,
spaces in the wrong parts of the face.
The arms are too thin and the eyes turn.

I'm found

America bursts with things it was never meant
to have. Take the fevers and accidents,
dark kitchen workers, crawling rafts.

LB²

Do you mean Save for the names? (except for.?)

But save the names, like mine.
Mine is different because it fits
on a normal typewriter,
because it knows,
because it is Adrienne.

Darkness, my name is & I'm almost ready to confess...

It's French.
It means artful.

Ironic... that you get away w/ this bold line is inexplicable & quite glorious.

Adrienne Su
April 13, 1989
Revision

Address

There are many ways of saying Chinese
in American. One means restaurant.
Others mean comprador, coolie, green army.

I've been practicing
how to walk and talk,
how to dress, what to do in a silk shop.

How to talk. America: Meiguo,
second tone and third.
The beautiful country.

In second grade we watched films
on King in Atlanta
and the ships at Old Gold Mountain.

They said we had hidden the Japanese
in California.
Everyone apologized to me.

But I am from Eldorado Drive in the suburbs.
There may be spaces
in the wrong parts of the face,

but America bursts with things it was never meant
to have. Take the fevers and accidents,
take the dark kitchen workers, crawling rafts.

But save the names, like mine.
It's different because it fits on a typewriter,
because it knows,

because it is Adrienne.
It's French.
It means artful.

Final version, as published in *Middle Kingdom:*

ADDRESS

There are many ways of saying Chinese
in American. One means restaurant.
Others mean comprador, coolie, green army.

I've been practicing
how to walk and talk,
how to dress, what to do in a silk shop.

How to talk. America: *Meiguo,*
second tone and third.
The beautiful country.

In second grade we watched films
on King in Atlanta.
How our nation was mistaken:

They said we had hidden the Japanese
in California.
Everyone apologized to me.

But I am from Eldorado Drive
in the suburbs. Sara Lee's
pound cake thaws in the heart

of the home, the parakeet bobs on a dowel,
night doesn't move. The slumber party
teems in its spot in the dark

summer; the swimming pool gleams.
Somewhere an inherited teapot is smashed
by a baseball. There may be spaces

in the wrong parts of the face,
but America bursts with things it was never meant
to have: the intent to outlast

the centerless acres,
the wedding cake tiered to heaven.
Every season a new crop of names,

like mine. It's different
because it fits on a typewriter,
because it's first in its line,

because it is Adrienne.
It's French.
It means *artful.*

Sometime after that first meeting, I met with Lucie at the Parad-
iso, a spacious, well-lit cafe that disappeared from Harvard Square
some years ago. Lucie had installed herself at a table for meetings
with students. She must have been interviewing for her course,
because I brought her a pile of poems. I was anxious to read all the
Asian American poets I could find, and as I talked about my journey to that category, which in today's context seems as obvious as
my trip back to English, Lucie said she felt similarly about being
a woman writing to a predominantly male tradition. The way she
said it was not dismissive; she genuinely felt like an interloper, too. I
wished, after our conversation, that the poems I had turned in were
more explicitly Asian American; most were racially unmarked. But

we ended up having plenty of opportunities to talk about those things.

My journal from that year mentions many phone calls from her, to suggest a poet to read (Li-Young Lee's first book, *Rose*, had just appeared, as had *The Forbidden Stitch: An Asian American Women's Anthology*, edited by Shirley Geok-lin Lim), or to remind me to attend a reading. While it's tempting to equate a phone call in 1989 with an email today, since the latter wasn't an option, they are not equivalent; the former took as much time and effort as it does today. At the time I didn't think to wonder whether Lucie was calling every student poet she knew. It seems impossible, but so do many of her achievements as both teacher and artist. Any time I have met other former students of hers, the same dreamy devotion comes up; we all seem to belong to a cult of Lucie. And it is thanks to one of her phone calls that I went to hear Rita Dove, Galway Kinnell, and Ellen Bryant Voigt one evening, and later ended up following Rita Dove to the University of Virginia, where, not incidentally, Lucie had studied as well. It is because of the author bio in Lucie's book, which listed a fellowship at the Fine Arts Work Center in Provincetown, that I set my sights on the Work Center, where I eventually spent a life-changing winter and met writers with whom I still exchange drafts and have shared many milestones.

Lucie's class became a form of weekly worship for me—not that the sessions were perfect or all students fully committed to the cause, but I always took my poems as far as I could on my own and was anxious for a response. I was writing often in meter and rhyme and cutting mercilessly, hoping for gleaming edges and heightened intensity. One week, I spent so many hours obsessing over a single comma that when I used my "author's chance to speak" after the workshop to ask about the comma, the class burst into laughter. So did I, once I realized what I'd been doing. Lucie inspired in us that perfectionism tempered with moments of sudden, self-aware levity. All that year, I kept going back to the only book she had pub-lished then—*A Hunger*, a collection suffused with loss, thwarted desire, and speakers in extreme circumstances, but not lacking in humor.

For instance, from "Autobiography":

> It is only three o'clock & already I'm alone
> Listening to the lovers next door
> Like Patsy Cline & her Man
> Throwing barebacked wooden furniture
> Like the real life bicker of true love.

The daring wink in the opulent, tragic "What the Whales Sound Like in Manhattan":

> It is a sound that catches on the canopies
> of pre-war highrise buildings designed to keep out
> light & Latin music & the seeds of Chinese children
>
> eating kiwis on these handsome summer nights.
> It is a sound that tips the gryphons on the tops
> of buildings, one that spreads the concrete wings
>
> of gargoyles clutched to rooftops looking out
> for seasons. In Manhattan it is not that common
> to have whales.

The confounding but hilarious aside in the ominous, otherworldly first poem in the collection, "Domestic Mysticism":

> When I come home, the dwarves will be long
> In their shadows & promiscuous. The alley cats will sneak
> Inside, curl about the legs of furniture, close the skins

Inside their eyelids, sleep. Orchids will be intercrossed &
    sturdy.
The sun will go down as I sit, thin armed, small breasted
In my cotton dress, poked with eyelet stitches, a little lace,
In the queer light left when a room snuffs out.

I draw a bath, enter the water as a god enters water:
Fertile, knowing, kind, surrounded by glass objects
Which could break easily if mishandled or ill-touched.
Everyone knows an unworshipped woman will betray you.

Overall, it was the extravagant and inevitable-feeling tragedy
that drew me to the poems, the four and a half pages spent in the
precocious head of "Jessica, from the Well," the extreme dysfunc-
tion of twin sisters who lose touch with reality and edge toward
violence in "Elective Mutes," the vague "you" who evokes an eco-
nomically and emotionally lost Midwest in "Ohio & Beyond." Lucie
could deploy the ampersand and the mid-sentence capital letter
with an authority I still can't muster myself; when I try either, the
effort looks amateur. I took *A Hunger* with me when I went home
on breaks. I kept consulting it for years afterward, whenever life
was cruel and inexplicable.

Lucie did not collect written comments from peer to peer but
trusted students to give them to each other, and for the most part,
everyone did. At the end of the term, Lucie told me that I would,
in the course of my writing life, "be criticized by people who can't
see the orchestration beneath the coolness of the poems' surfaces."
As I think she did for everyone, she gave me a handwritten letter
in response to my portfolio at the end of the term. Over the years I
have read and reread this letter, loving the distinctive, loopy hand-
writing that had skated all over my drafts, usually in three colors.

The letter gave me the strength to persist in the face of the routine rejection that all but the most blessed of writers face.

Some excerpts:

> I am certain, long since, that you are the Real Item. I've got this Faith (I've got this mystic streak in me . . .).
>
> More & more, week by week, I am convinced of this . . . It *is* my business to encourage, enlighten, entertain, support—but I am not Merely encouraging you. I mean more than that. I know your Gift. It's real & Genetic & true . . .
>
> Here's the thing:
>
> I am, as you know, drawn often to the garish . . . the risky, the Bold, the Audacious, the long-winded, the High-winded. Drawn to *that*. And what delights me *most* about your work is how enormously coolblooded it is. Sometimes, nearly Bloodless. And so it shocks & astounds me! That these qualities of near-tepid detachment, of near-compulsive tightness, of lukewarmness in the poems draws (& gives off) such heat. Small miracle? This is the gift.
>
> . . . Get thee to a Nunnery.
>
> Get thee to a Garrett.

Because she did not collect the written comments, she had no way of knowing that I was already receiving, on occasion, the criticism she warned about, although some classmates must surely have vocalized them in workshop. There was praise, but someone called my use of form "oppressive" and urged me to abandon it; another said the poems had no emotion and could I add some? This is indeed the risk of imposing a lot of discipline on a poem: withhold a hair too much, and rather than concentrating a feeling, you end up obscuring it. But if it was coming through to Lucie, maybe I was on to something.

For a couple of years after graduation, I wrote letters to Lucie, sent poems, and sometimes called. I had moved to New York, where I loved the racial and linguistic diversity and unlimited literary events, but where I spent my days in a cubicle, had about ten dollars per week from my paycheck to spend on something other than necessities, and could not find community; outside poetry, I was miserable. She called and wrote back, although she warned on a cat postcard I still have: "Forgive me for not writing back always & quickly—but know I think of you, reading your letters with pleasure. Don't let New York drive you mad—it wd. me. This is why I live here in the beauty of the Provinces." When I made my first application to the Fine Arts Work Center, Lucie warned that my age, which would have been twenty-two or twenty-three, was going to work against me; she had gone at twenty-four and found herself the youngest person there. Indeed, the Work Center describes itself as a place for emerging artists who have finished their formal training, and I had not yet been to graduate school. I was impatient, although not nearly as impatient as Lucie, who had been declared "audacious" by an early teacher, to whom she had submitted an eighty-three-page poem. Another of her teachers, Charles Wright, who would also become my teacher, told me he wasn't sure he had "taught" Lucie anything: she had, he said, come to UVa already on her own self-made trajectory. I called her when the Work Center's rejection letter arrived with a handwritten sentence at the bottom: "The Committee admired your work." Without hesitation, Lucie said, "That means they are going to accept you later," which ensured that I would keep applying. Plus, now that I have served on that selection committee, I know how rare such a note is; she was not "Merely encouraging" me but speaking on authority.

I don't know how she managed to stay in touch, because there

were so many of us, more every year, and while not everyone
intended to become a poet, the affection seemed universal. On the
last day of our workshop, when the students sat silently filling out
course evaluation forms with Lucie out of the room, someone had
broken the silence with the remark, "How can we fill these things
out? It's like critiquing your own mother," and that same withheld
laughter—as after the comma question—filled the room. That
habit of withholding, then letting go, was a behavior she had cultivated in us; she projected formality in class, then broke it with an
outrageous, hilarious remark—and this too was a lesson in writing
well.

I don't love going to Target, but sometimes it's the best place to
shop, for those days when you would otherwise have to go to four
separate stores, needing, say, a shower curtain, a workout top, a
pen refill, and a lemon. Not much of a poet when it comes to caf-
feine, I bypass the Starbucks. But since Lucie's untimely death, Target—this Target—has taken on a certain sanctity for me. I think
of Lucie as the automatic doors open to let me in, and again to let
me out. I wonder where in the huge parking lot we packed her loot
for its journey to the legendary apartment in New York, where her
Columbia students were lucky enough to meet for workshops. I
think of her negotiating the "real world" of tollbooths and dentists,
that world she renounced as fully as possible to spend her life in
poetry, and she seems—especially under the spell of her poems—a
person loaned to us from another universe. I think of her Victorian-
clad radiance every week in that class nearly thirty years ago and
her graciousness in later coming to Dickinson for what must have
been much less than her normal honorarium, as a kindness to me.
I remember the day she came to workshop and complained that a
boot had been put on her car; she was occupied with higher things
than when to move the car, trivia that clutters the heads of us com-
moners, and literature is the better for it. I think with gratitude

of that reception in 1988: what would my life look like if I, or she, hadn't attended? And I hear in my head certain passages from that book I carried around like a talisman in the early years and finally thought to have autographed in 2006, in case it would be a long time until we met again:

> If I have something important to say
> I hope I live here long enough
> To say it gracefully. The wind moves
> Everything. Nothing is exempt.
>> — from "Magnum Mysterium"

> Now you're gone too & that's one more
> Of us who won't go ragging into old age.
>> — from "A Little Piece of Everlasting Life"

> The earth opens for me
> as I always knew it would for a wish.
>> — from "Jessica, from the Well"

2018

Permission Not to Go

M Y LITERARY SENSIBILITY was formed mainly in cities, but like many poets who teach full-time, I find, at mid-career, that I have spent most of my adult life in a small town, in my case, Carlisle, Pennsylvania. Early on, as a twentysomething aspiring poet in New York City, where I felt most like my true self but could not find a job that fit, I knew I might end up somewhere rural. But the prospect was abstract, and conditions developed gradually.

Dickinson College (named not after Emily but John), where I teach, contributes to its surroundings in the same way most colleges far from urban centers do. It hosts free concerts, art shows, panel discussions, and literary events; supplies space for a food bank; and voluntarily pays real-estate taxes. It supports community efforts to protect air quality and waterways, as Carlisle sits at the intersection of two major highways and has become the site for a large number of Amazon warehouses. And the college draws guest speakers, students, and faculty from all over the nation and world, enriching daily life.

At the same time, the town-gown divide is palpable. Every fall, our students clog the limited street parking, often in expensive vehicles with Connecticut or New York plates. Many faculty members flee as soon as classes end, if they don't already live elsewhere; Baltimore and Philadelphia are challenging but not impossible commutes. For most it is because their families live far away, their spouses can't find work here, and/or because their research requires travel, but it would be false to deny that it's also because many have dismissed the town as provincial. Despite efforts to adapt, we bemoan the narrow range of restaurants and their short-sighted use of Styrofoam to-go containers, buy pricey organic food, and hold up cultural events to the urban standard. When recruiting new colleagues, we always make the case that Carlisle is "only three and a half hours" from New York City, implicitly affirming that there is nothing here.

I plead guilty to many of these offenses. I read more national and international than local news, spend a relative fortune on food, drive a Prius, and almost always have a plane ticket for some date in the near future. I relish my time in cities.

Yet my travel is almost always for work or family; it is seldom a getaway. My more exalted food shopping is mostly from local farmers. Running a household alone with children and pets, I do a tremendous amount of unpaid domestic labor year-round and as a result can never spend more than about three hours in an ivory tower. The way I spend my time is reflected in the outward subject matter of some of my poems, especially my most recent book, *Living Quarters*, which focuses on four regions of a house.

In my eighteen years here, I've had three sabbaticals. Watching colleagues rent out their houses to take sabbaticals in far-flung places, I have spent all of mine in this borough of 18,500, away from the worldly pleasures of New York or even Philadelphia, except for short trips.

In part, joint custody has forced me to do this, and perhaps when my kids are grown, I'll go away, too, but—aside from the fact that it is much harder to get funding to make up the salary cut—staying put has never seemed a bad artistic choice. Instead of house-hunting, finding new schools and doctors, preparing the house for renters, and moving, I get to start writing the minute I post final grades.

While I have certainly worried that any woman poet who writes more than a few poems on domestic topics—cooking, gardening, buying groceries—is likely to be marginalized, Emily Dickinson has always been a pillar in my head, making the best argument for the potential profundity of mundane topics, as well as the irrelevance of the poet's demographics, if the poems are strong.

"A narrow Fellow in the grass"; "A Bird, came down the Walk –"; "The Bat is dun, with wrinkled Wings –"; "She sights a Bird – she chuckles –"; "The Sky is low – the Clouds are mean –"; "The morns are meeker than they were –" all seem to have taken place in Dickinson's backyard in Amherst. Poems such as these remind me that what I crave is available right here, and while I treasure the chance to seek inspiration in a world-class museum or the restaurant of a famous chef, there is no excuse for not simply going outside for it, when more exalted things are out of reach.

Behind my house, in an unkempt yard, appear many of the same entities through which Dickinson reveals the universe: bees, a robin, worms, a neighbor's cat, squirrels, flies, butterflies, clover, dew, spiders, sunlight, snow, even a few inadvertent roses.

The Dickinson poem that gives me heart in this context is not particularly about flora or fauna, although it contains a little of each:

236

Some – keep the Sabbath – going to church –
I – keep it – staying at Home –
With a Bobolink – for a Chorister –
And an Orchard – for a Dome –

Some – keep the Sabbath, in Surplice –
I – just wear my wings –
And instead of tolling the bell, for church –
Our little Sexton – sings –

"God" – preaches – a noted Clergyman –
And the sermon is never long,
So – instead of getting to Heaven – at last –
I'm – going – all along!

In my take on this poem, the townspeople are a population of intellectuals and artists. Everyone is seeking not after God but intellectual and creative fruition. The "church" is every site of ostensible worldliness: urban centers, prestigious conferences, the inner circles of leaders in every field. To "keep the Sabbath," as I read the poem in my current context, is to create something of potentially lasting value.

Dickinson's poem criticizes worshipers who think spirituality can be found only in the outer forms of the church ("a Chorister," "a Dome," "Surplice," "the bell," "the sermon") and affirms her independent path toward God. Able to worship "staying at Home," she has several advantages over them: She doesn't have to put on her Sunday best, the Sexton (a bird) is right outside her house, she doesn't have to endure lengthy sermons, and most of all, she doesn't have to wait until death to "[get] to Heaven." Instead, she is "going – all along!"

That last line shouts gleefully, its solitary triumph made unsolitary by faith in its future readers. Its speaker seems to know that someday her iconoclasm will be vindicated, even embraced, and that the fashions of literary publishing are temporary. It reminds me that the highest truths are accessible wherever you are, if you can shed your assumptions about what constitutes worldliness, then open your mind at just the right angle.

2018

· 3 ·

The Poet and the Poem

Gifts to the Future: Notes on Section Three

WHEN MY FRIEND Claire Kageyama-Ramakrishnan passed away in her prime in 2016, I first thought about her husband and daughter, then about all the poems that would never be written. Later, in conversation with others who knew and loved her, I shifted my focus to celebrating the poems she wrote in her too-brief time on Earth.

True to the rest of this volume, different types of writing come together here: personal as well as analytical writing about Claire Kageyama-Ramakrishnan; a close reading of a poem by Carol Ann Duffy; and a review of a book on Asian American poetics.

That review—of *Thinking Its Presence: Form, Race, and Subjectivity in Contemporary Asian American Poetry* by Dorothy Wang— exists because, in the early 1990s, I fell into the poetry-slam scene at the Nuyorican Poets Café in New York City's East Village, where Steve Cannon, writer, professor, gallery owner, and publisher, was a beloved heckler. Many years later, in 2017 and 2018, I occasionally reviewed books for Steve's magazine *A Gathering of the Tribes*.

In 2017, when I read in the neighborhood, at KGB Bar, Steve, who had since lost his sight completely, attended. It was the first time I had seen him since my Nuyorican days. It was also the last; he passed away in 2019 at the age of 84, having inspired and brought together dozens of Lower East Side artists and writers.

Rest in peace, Steve. Rest in peace, Claire.

Foreword to *Vidya's Tree* by Claire Kageyama-Ramakrishnan

V*IDYA'S TREE* opens with the phrase "When I was young" and closes with "*We're in Heaven—it's this beautiful garden.*"

Claire could not have intended the resonance with the context in which this chapbook appears. Her illness and death came quickly and unexpectedly, in the prime of her working life. Healthy and in her mid-forties, she was balancing a heavy teaching load, the raising of a young daughter, and the writing of her third book-length manuscript, not a chapbook of Final Poems.

As her grieving friend, I now isolate those phrases for my own purposes. I selfishly read "When I was young" as that two-year period in our early twenties when Claire and I were MFA candidates in creative writing at the University of Virginia, and take "Heaven" to be the "beautiful garden" in which Claire might now be enjoying a Satsuma orange tree with her parents. In context, of course, these are not what the phrases describe. "When I was young" refers to the poet's childhood, and "*We're in Heaven—it's this beautiful garden*" imagines the poet's deceased parents trying to speak to their living daughter. But the pleasure of poetry is that lines can do double duty, serving both the reader's and writer's purposes, and I'm sure Jon Loomis and Rajesh Ramakrishnan placed these bookends with this doubleness in mind.

I see those two years at UVa as the youth of Claire's career. She had just graduated from college and was able to make poetry the center of her life for the first time. She and I spent lengthy days and nights talking about poetry and our hopes for the future. We imagined who we might become as poets, where we might publish our first books, and how subject matter might come to mark us. Both American-born but having ongoing experiences shaped by race, we wondered to what extent we should write about Japan and China, countries more foreign than familiar, yet significant in ways we felt compelled to explore. What would become of us if we did or didn't address them? We conjectured about where we might end up living and how much writing time might be available in responsible adulthood. We also did our best to seize the present, often through the shared pleasures of cooking and eating, but our young ages and student status forced us to be future-oriented.

A quarter-century later, entrenched in responsible adulthood, I write after a different two years, two years of awareness that Claire is gone from the planet. Since the shock of her death, my daily life has not been much different on the surface—we lived many miles apart and had not been in regular touch over the years—but Claire was and is a lasting part of my creative foundation. Over the decades, sitting down to write or read, I felt assured by the knowledge that she was depicting the landscapes of her native L.A., asking tough questions about family, and imaginatively inhabiting the visual art she loved. I could hear her, in my head, setting me straight when I started second-guessing my drafts. Now I imagine her doing so from that "beautiful garden."

That is, I am forced to look backward where, with Claire, I used to look forward. Reading *Vidya's Tree*, I see the maturation of her longtime fascination with Frida Kahlo; the resolution of those early struggles with subject matter in "After the Earthquake and Tsunami, 2011"; her knowledge of meter and rhyme fully integrated into her deployment of free verse; and her gift for plain statement brought to an apex in "The Backyard Garden in Houston," constructed entirely of end-stopped lines, each its own sentence. These poems, like all good poems, are gifts to the future. The tragedy is that the future came so soon. I hope this collection will be gratefully received not only by Claire's existing readers but also by many who are hearing her voice for the first time, as well as by others who will hear it in another era, perhaps after all of us are gone.

2019

Saturday Morning: Remembering
Claire Kageyama-Ramakrishnan

TWENTY-FIVE years ago, when Claire Kageyama-Ramakrishnan and I became classmates in the MFA program in poetry at the University of Virginia, we were the only Asian Americans in our cohort; a third, Roy Kamada, would join us the next year. Both in our twenties, Claire and I were tangling with the role of Asian American identity in our literary lives. Could we have our say about it and move on, or would it follow us throughout our careers? Could we sometimes pretend it wasn't there? Would we be pigeonholed if we didn't? Would people at cocktail parties ever stop bringing up Amy Tan?

Claire understood the difficult negotiations required every time one of our poems addressed family history, used Chinese or Japanese words, had characters who were Asian American but not explicitly identified as such, or invoked ugly American immigration laws. We talked about them at length and tried to help each other find the right balance between the personal and the political. Having moved to Charlottesville from Los Angeles and New York City respectively, we also missed Asian foods and cooked them as well as we could, trading occasional recipes along with poem drafts.

After UVa, we inadvertently lost touch. We went to opposite coasts, she to Berkeley, I to Provincetown. We both eventually acquired teaching jobs, pets, homes, families. But Claire's sudden death this spring at the age of forty-six made me realize that she was still with me—a continuing influence, through all she had said and done when we were classmates. And in her mature poems, I see the fruition of what she was working on twenty-five years ago; I only wish there were another twenty-five, or fifty, years of her poems to look forward to.

Claire's poem "Shuumatsu: American Born Japanese" from her second collection, *Bear, Diamonds and Crane*, reads to me as a deepening of some of those early conversations. It is at peace with its hybrid identity. It knows when to use the Japanese word, when the English. Ensconced in a collection with formal range, it confidently asserts its shape. Deftly wielding the personal and political, it both announces itself and feels naturally occurring, as if the reader had dropped in on the speaker on a weekend morning.

The poem creates a setting so domestic that the reader knows almost nothing about what lies outside the house—or even outside the kitchen. At first glance, it seems to be an affectionate catalogue of breakfast foods that happen to be Japanese. The poem is short enough to include in full:

SHUUMATSU[1]: AMERICAN BORN JAPANESE

Early morning breakfast. Scrambled eggs,
chopsticks, scallions, soy sauce, steamed rice,
or last night's leftover rice. Jar of pickled
daikon, *Takuan*. I like the kind from
Maui, mild or spicy, with sprinkled chilies
floating in sweet brine. I like breakfast
with a dab of sweet *nori*—sticky seaweed
seasoned with salted mushrooms, bonito.

---

1. Shuumatsu is Japanese for weekend. [Poet's footnote.]

Green tea and brown rice tea leaves swirl
in squat *chawan*—glazed cup. My Maine Coon
grooms his tail stripes on the window ledge
near a succulent tangerine, ripe fruit
left for the gods. This is heaven, or close
to it. This is my life on Saturday.

I think of this poem as a distant cousin of Jane Kenyon's "Otherwise," which also describes a breakfast: "I ate / cereal, sweet / milk, ripe, flawless / peach," then goes on to list quotidian events—walking the dog, lying down "with my mate"—with restrained reverence. Both poems highlight the transience of simple pleasures. Both are written in plain language and free verse. Both invoke two worlds: the here and now, described in food and daily activities, and the hereafter (in Kenyon, "one day, I know, it will be otherwise"; in Kageyama-Ramakrishnan, "This is heaven, or close / to it"). That both poets died at approximately the same early age is just terrible, terrible luck; the poems would be kin regardless.

What makes Claire's poem particularly layered is the contrast it draws between the private world of the kitchen and the public world of migration across continents. While the poem's closedness to the outdoors prevents us from seeing anything in the speaker's yard (if indeed there is a yard), or learning what she does from Monday to Friday, we can identify in the list of breakfast foods an unbroken link to her Japanese ancestry. While perhaps a significant proportion of the American population has eaten Japanese (or nominally Japanese) food in the States, for most, it's probably been in a restaurant, for dinner or lunch. Breakfast, on the other hand, is the true test of identity. The most intimate meal, the least likely to be eaten with company, it reflects the eater's genuine tastes, especially when—despite starting with the mainstream-sounding "Scrambled eggs"—it includes "scallions, soy sauce, steamed rice, / or last night's leftover rice," pickles, and dried, seasoned seaweed.

As the speaker rhapsodizes about "chilies / floating in sweet brine" and the umami-rich "*nori*—sticky seaweed / seasoned with salted mushrooms, bonito," we're drawn into her appetite and forget that waffles exist. For this speaker, and for the reader who is persuaded, the traditional American divide between breakfast foods and lunch/dinner foods collapses. We become, momentarily, the "American Born Japanese" of the title.

And yet, the phrase "American Born Japanese" jars. It has fallen out of use and been replaced by "Japanese American" for good reasons. "American Born Japanese" implies that being racially Japanese excludes one from being American. It turns an American of Japanese descent into a Japanese person who happened to be born in America, even if she is *yonsei*, fourth-generation (which the speaker's child is, in the book's final poem). This is a pernicious assumption that legitimizes shameful policies like the World War II internment of Japanese Americans, which, the collection reveals, directly affected the poet's family. That the title provocatively uses the phrase "American Born Japanese," along with the Japanese rather than English word for "weekend," suggests a wholehearted but occasional embrace of Japanese identity, alongside the ongoing struggle of Asian Americans to be acknowledged as fully American. It's a way of announcing that, on Saturday, the speaker has the time and privacy to be as Japanese as she likes—and by reading the surrounding poems, we understand why being more Japanese might require privacy.

At the same time, the poem italicizes, and pauses to translate, several Japanese words for the reader: *takuan, nori, chawan*. Aware that its audience is unlikely to know the words, the poem makes this explicit effort to include the reader, at some risk (averted, I believe) of disrupting the line. The smooth integration of definitions not only serves a practical purpose but also shows that the speaker is accustomed to having to explain aspects of her life, and does so almost automatically.

Meanwhile, the life depicted is clearly American, and not just in the title. The two place names are American: Maui, Maine. The cat, the only living thing in the poem apart from the speaker, is a Maine Coon, a breed associated—in legend if not fact—with New England's early European settlers. And the centrality of the breakfast description means it is noteworthy: the speaker knows it is not what the neighbors are eating, nor is it what the speaker herself eats during the work week. She is just like the neighbors—except when she isn't.

Although it could decide to be annoyed, the poem focuses on pleasure: the quiet delight of a leisurely Saturday morning, enhanced by the knowledge that Sunday morning is yet to come. And it does so in fourteen lines, as if to say, I could have made this a tanka or haiku cycle, but how about a sonnet, or the shape of one? On weekend mornings, forms can be worn casually.

If memory serves, I had an actual breakfast with Claire only once, when I was getting ready to move and needed a place to stay for one night. Claire put me up in her apartment. I'm pretty sure it was a Sunday night, so we must have had Monday breakfast together, probably a typical start-of-the-week one: bagels? cereal? toast and fruit? I can't remember. As the saying goes, life fades while art endures. Through her poetry, Claire has made a breakfast that's unforgettable to me and, I hope, to many who never met her.

2018

A Tribute to
Claire Kageyama-Ramakrishnan

Association of Writers & Writing Programs
Conference Panel, March 9, 2018

CLAIRE AND I were at UVa together, from 1991 to 1993, in the MFA program in poetry. I felt an affinity with her poems early on, but our friendship developed more gradually, in the way that long friendships often do. Which is why I regret that we lost touch afterwards—not from any conscious decision on either side, I believe, but because we went to opposite coasts, both moved around a lot, and both needed to balance the demands of career and family. I now know that I made the basic human mistake of assuming we would meet again. I think we do that especially with people we know to be dependable—the friends you can pick up with wherever you left off.

It's a gift to us that Claire was so devoted to poetry because her poems will stay with those of us who knew her, just as they reside with readers who did not know her, and will lodge themselves with future readers not born in time to know her. But Claire's creativity was not exclusive to poetry. Claire was also a resourceful and energetic home cook. Where writing strives to produce something permanent that reaches readers far removed in space and time (readers we all, in workshops, try to imagine), cooking produces something fleeting that touches people in the immediate vicinity, but it is not lesser for that. That's why it's important to me today to remember her culinary skill and imagination along with her writing.

During graduate school, I kept sporadic journals, which is how I know, a quarter-century later, that on January 14, 1992, Claire and I saw the film *JFK*, then went to her apartment, where she proceeded to make a chocolate cake while we talked. Who starts baking *after* an evening movie? Graduate students; people who want a languorous evening of conversation. The cake wasn't ready until midnight. We often talked until late, much later than that sometimes; some of my journal entries are marked "4 a.m.—Claire just left." Claire's enthusiasm about baking—her readiness to just start spontaneously—often gave us an additional excuse to linger. My journals are terrible reading—cesspools of doubt in shapeless semi-paragraphs—but I am thankful to them for letting me know now that on December 7, 1992, Claire and I went from workshop to my house, where I cooked noodles with chicken and bean sprouts, plus oshitashi, for our dinner. Both of us had baked for workshop that day, so we also ate some of the cookies she had contributed to class. She had also made a homemade cream cheese pie, and I had made apple-banana bread, both of which we delivered to our professor, Greg Orr, ahead of class, but for some reason neither was served and we never got them back. I hope that Greg—whose mentorship Claire cherished and talked about all the time—took them home to his family and they became part of his narrative, whether remembered or forgotten today. Here in 2018, I take real pleasure in knowing that on January 10, 1993, after Claire and I went to the gym together, she made us this lunch: salad with broiled tuna, tomato-basil biscuits, banana milkshakes. Why did I write that down in 1993? It was a gift. It was going to matter someday, beyond that lunch.

Other food memories, I did not record, but they have lingered with me. One morning, Claire and I—but mostly Claire—made a pound cake at her place. She brought it to workshop and gave me credit, even though she had done almost everything. At some point, a new kind of grocery store arrived in Charlottesville: Fresh Fields, which was similar to Whole Foods and equally expensive. What helped make up for the prices was that the store was constantly giving out free samples. Claire and I routinely walked up and down the aisles, eating the samples and taking the little recipe sheets offered along with them. I think we sometimes went to Fresh Fields even when we didn't need to shop.

Claire had come to Charlottesville from Los Angeles, right after graduating from college. In her first year at UVa, I was the only other Asian American in the program, so she voiced to me some of her culture shock. "Where are the Asians?" she asked me more than once as we walked through town, passing burger joints, pizza parlors, and packs of mostly white sorority or fraternity members. Both of us longed for Asian food, which was hard to find except in the small-town-American style. Anticipating this, I had moved to Charlottesville with a full pantry bought in New York Chinatown, and while I remember that just about anything I cooked was welcomed by hungry classmates, I appreciated having Claire there to share my enthusiasm for the weirder stuff, like red bean desserts. I remember seeing on her bookshelf the same two genres that occupy most of mine: poetry and cookbooks. She had Gloria Bley Miller's *Thousand Recipe Chinese Cookbook*, several Japanese cookbooks, and some mainstream American ones, which, given our location, were the easiest to cook from. Those books affirmed not only something shared about our Asian Americanness but also our shared love of cooking.

One of our first excursions together was to a restaurant called Ming Dynasty; I remember nothing about the restaurant but must have found its name important enough to record. Our mutual feeling of partial exile transferred to our writing, in which both of us were trying to figure out how to write about our families: what to reveal or conceal, how to handle injustice, how to deal with race.

Claire's family history, as depicted in her poems about the World War II internment of Japanese Americans, gave her plenty of reasons to be enraged, but she was vigilant about avoiding political rhetoric and simplistic emotion. Sometimes she felt pressed, by the workshop conversation, to take a polemical route, and that became something we dissected later while cooking or eating or both. Both of us were cautious about writing about family history for another reason: *The Joy Luck Club* had recently come out, and it was the only Asian American literary work most people had read. Much as we wanted Asian American stories to be told, we almost felt that we individually would be better off without it, because pre-*Joy Luck*, people had not assumed they already knew all about us. It may have been worse for Claire than for me because she was not even Chinese American, yet in the popular imagination, Chinese and Japanese characters were conflated. One of my earliest memories of Claire is of her fury at being told by a stranger, "You look just like Amy Tan!" Claire told me she had glared back, not because Amy Tan was unattractive but because it appeared that Asian American women writers could never escape the comparison. We laughed together about incidents like this all the time, but when it came to shaping poems, Claire was intense and serious. It was no surprise to me, decades later, to see how judiciously she handled the topic of internment.

That is why I would like to close by reading a section of her long poem "Shadow Mountain," the title poem from her first book.

6. ONE QUESTION, SEVERAL ANSWERS

Where did your father live?
  House on Federal, City of Angels.

Where did your father live?
  Horse stall at a racetrack.

Where did your father live?
> *Near the aqueduct, in a man-made desert.*

Where did your father live?
> *By a pear tree.*
> *With pears, ripe pears from that tree.*

Where did your father live?
> *Block 25.*

Where did your father live?
> *With thin strips of tarpaper.*
> *Pot under his straw mattress.*

Where did your father live?
> *Waiting in line to use the latrines.*
> *Waiting in line at the mess hall.*
> *Waiting for his parents.*

Where did your father live?
> *The Desert Chapel.*

Where did your father live?
> *With his brothers,*
> *transplants—Joshua trees.*

Where did your father live?
> *In his mother's heart.*

Where did your father live?
> *Barrack 12, Unit 3.*

Where did your father live?
> *With 5 strand barbs.*
> *With windstorms and bitterbrush.*
> *With years of snowmelt, glacial erasure.*

2018

Book Review: *Thinking Its Presence: Form, Race, and Subjectivity in Contemporary Asian American Poetry* by Dorothy Wang

E VERY NOW and then, an Asian American student asks me, "Should I write about race? It's important to me and I want to, but I'm afraid I'll be pigeonholed."

I always think it through on the spot, to make sure I still agree with myself. Among my answers: "Poetry is such an obscure genre, it's not worth doing anything but what means the most to you." Or: "Robert Frost said a poem begins as a lump in the throat. Without that, your poems will lack urgency, so write about what's eating at you." Or: "Look at what's happening politically, all over the Western world. Open racism is back. Your story needs to be told."

Until I read Dorothy J. Wang's *Thinking Its Presence: Form, Race, and Subjectivity in Contemporary Asian American Poetry* (Stanford University Press, 2014), I never considered what to say about choosing *not* to write about race. It didn't occur to me to say, "If race is something you want to write about but you rarely address it outright, and you make a name for yourself as a poet, the apparent absence of race in your work will be used to prove that race doesn't matter. Your work will be pitted against the work of other poets of color who happen to write about race, to denigrate them."

Examining five Chinese American poets and their critical reception—Li-Young Lee, Marilyn Chin, John Yau, Mei-Mei Berssenbrugge, and Pamela Lu—Wang's book covers a wide range of aesthetics. The critical trends most prominently addressed are the tendency to reduce lyric poets of Asian descent to their Asian Americanness ("content"), and to reduce Asian American avant-garde poets to their style ("form"), their racial interrogations minimized or ignored. Wang includes a compelling endnote explaining why all of the poets featured in this "Asian American" study are Chinese American. Among her reasons: the Chinese language and Chinese American history are in Wang's area of expertise, Chinese Americans are the oldest and largest group of Asian Americans, and this statement:

> I see no fundamental differences between the issues faced by Chinese American poets and those faced by other Asian American ones. Just as Asian Americans tend to be seen as "all looking alike" in the popular imaginary, Asian American writers are generally viewed as monolithically and homogeneously "Asian" in the academic and literary realms. Understanding the shared and similar history of racial interpellation and mistreatment in the United States and of efforts by those in the Asian American movement of the late 1960s and early 1970s to forge strategic alliances and political identities based on these shared histories, I am convinced that my choice of the more general term "Asian American" is apt—even necessary—for the logic and larger implications of my arguments (323).

This rationale is in itself an argument against the division of "content" from "form." As long as Asian Americans—whether as poets or as people on the street—are "seen as 'all looking alike' in the popular imaginary," poetry cannot be the "postidentity" art, free of the irritating consideration of race, that some want it to be.

Underlying Wang's literary arguments are some of the darkest moments in Asian American history, including the Chinese Exclusion Act, labor abuses, anti-miscegenation laws, the internment of Japanese Americans, and the murder of Vincent Chin, along with the continuing perception of Asian Americans as foreign. In one of many tantalizing endnotes, Wang, a professor of American Studies, tells a personal anecdote that will be familiar to any Asian American: "I was once asked by an Ivy League professor of philosophy whether English was my native language, though he had heard my completely American accent and knew I was an English professor; before I could even respond, he answered his own (rhetorical) question: 'I think not'" (320).

Wang makes the case that the maligned topic of identity is of continuing relevance not just to Asian American poets and critics of Asian American poetry, but to everyone who writes and reviews American poetry. To ignore the possibility of race as a factor in an Asian American poet's sensibility, even when the poet does not address it directly, is as glib as that person you meet at parties who proclaims, "I don't see race!" Even when reading white poets, Wang argues, race is worth considering among the elements that shaped the artist. Robert Lowell is brought up more than once as an example: being white and from Massachusetts has an effect on a poet's use of language. Wang's point, that everyone has race, should not be controversial, yet it seems to underlie much of the political turmoil that the nation (not just its literary critics) finds itself in. To attribute race to every poet, instead of only the nonwhite ones, is the only way to end the implicit division of literature into "real" versus "ethnic" and give everyone a fair read. Yet, as Wang explains, a number of prominent critics seem to want to believe—despite the racially marked experience any American of color can describe—that no one has race.

"Ethnic" is a problematic word when used to describe people of color exclusively, since the usage is based on the assumption that whiteness is the human norm and therefore unmarked, whereas all other races have this quality called "ethnicity" that makes them something other than just plain human. While Wang uses the term "ethnic" in this way and I find it a little grating, it is done in the service of one day wiping out the assumptions on which it operates. Also, it is still in use in many institutions and there is not yet, to my knowledge, a suitable replacement.

Thinking Its Presence covers not only poets of various aesthetics but also poets who have different reputations concerning politics. Marilyn Chin is seen (and self-described) as political, while John Yau is generally perceived as minimally political, perhaps even apolitical. Yau's career illustrates the struggles of a poet whose work defies most categorization to navigate critical expectations, with the added complication of belonging to a minority race: "For decades, Yau never quite fit any poetic category—Language, avant-garde, cultural nationalist, ethnic, postmodernist, conceptual, among others—and, to some extent, still does not." Associated with the mainly white New York School, Yau said in an interview that "I don't feel a part of it" (167), and that early in his career, other Asian American poets viewed his work as "not Asian enough" (167). The frequent absence of an explicit self in Yau's poems is largely read as "a generic postmodern move" (181), but both Wang's analysis and Yau's interview statements make clear that the literary effacement of the self can express a value common to Chinese American families: the non-primacy of the individual. A Chinese American poet might well write from a point of view other than "I" for reasons of upbringing, without labeling that perspective as Chinese American. A thoughtful reader will neither force that interpretation on every Chinese American poet nor dismiss the possibility wholesale, but examine the work with an informed and open mind.

Another mystery concerning Yau's image as non-political is that Yau famously took critic and translator Eliot Weinberger to task in

1994 for largely excluding poets of color from the 1993 anthology *American Poetry Since 1950: Innovators and Outsiders*. In a vicious exchange that unfolded in *American Poetry Review*, Yau's activism was denounced as mercenary because his previous body of work did not explicitly champion the same causes. He was even criticized for not speaking Chinese, as if that undermined his authority as an Asian American.

In fact, beginning with *Radiant Silhouette* (including, of course, poems written before the book's publication in 1989), Yau was interrogating stereotypes of Asian American men by creating a fictional character, Genghis Chan, who combines elements of two figures from popular culture, Charlie Chan and Genghis Khan, "the 'good,' submissive Oriental (Charlie Chan, the houseboy) and the 'evil' Oriental, represented by the barbaric invader (Genghis Khan) or the devious despot (Fu Manchu) or a combination of the two (Ming the Merciless)" (219-20). The Genghis Chan poems continue over several subsequent books. Wang devotes an entire chapter to Genghis Chan and notes that "...many white experimental poets and poetry critics, while embracing Yau's style, tend to ignore discussing poems such as those in the Genghis Chan series" (232). These points are valuable. They have the potential not only to encourage experimental poets and critics to more fully acknowledge race in literary works, but also to help more nonwhite readers and writers find relevance in experimental poetry.

Meanwhile, Marilyn Chin's more straightforward politics do not seem to get her into trouble when they appear in poems; it's only when Chin ventures to make a statement in (unambiguously nonfiction) prose that she runs into open hostility. Perhaps, Wang writes, the genre of poetry gives the reader enough leeway to dismiss a political position as not quite meaning what it says, or as not applying to this particular reader. Wang recounts a heated exchange that appeared in the Letters section of *Poetry* magazine in

2008, over Chin's translation of a poem by Ho Xuan Huong, a Viet-namese woman poet of the eighteenth century. Wang's analysis of the letters, Chin's response, and further responses to Chin show that words do not function in the same way for everyone; a reader or writer must weigh the complexities of who is saying and receiving them, to determine whether they have racial implications. I can see why some of the letter writers whose words offended Chin thought their remarks were free of racism. I can also see the racial (and unintentional) undertones Chin saw. Most Americans already know from daily life that the same spoken remark can have different implications when said by a white person to a person of color, by a white person to another white person, by a person of color to a white person, between two people of color of the same race, between two people of color of different races, and so on, and they adjust their speech accordingly. Ironically, people sometimes see the printed word as bulletproof where they might intuit that the spoken word is not. By examining the *Poetry* exchange in-depth, *Thinking Its Presence* can help the well-intentioned improve.

Another achievement of the book is its connecting of poets who seem to have nothing—aside from Chinese Americanness—in common. Aesthetically, Li-Young Lee, whose work is often called Romantic and who has gained perhaps the most popular acceptance of all the poets examined in the book, could not be farther, formally, from Pamela Lu and Mei-Mei Berssenbrugge. But one thing Lee shares with Lu and Berssenbrugge is that readers often assume that they abstain—mostly—from "identity politics," while allegedly lesser Asian American poets are dismissed as nursing grievances.

Yet, in parsing Lee's famous long poem "The Cleaving," in which the speaker observes a Chinese butcher at a meat counter, Wang demonstrates meaningful engagement with questions of identity—engagement that should be self-evident but has sometimes been deliberately overlooked. Here is one of several passages Wang cites, from among the many associations the speaker brings to his reflections on the butcher (Wang 86):

> and the standing deaths
> at the counters, in the aisles,
> the walking deaths in the streets,
> the death-far-from-home, the death-
> in-a-strange-land, these Chinatown
> deaths, these American deaths.

Wang also reminds us that this poem cites racist writings about Asians by Ralph Waldo Emerson, and that another well-known Lee poem, "Persimmons," portrays an apparently autobiographical incident, in which a white American teacher physically punishes a Chinese immigrant child for confusing the words persimmon and precision. In addition, by analyzing Lee's evolving use of metaphor, Wang refutes both the judgment that Lee's poems are not political—his own intentions notwithstanding—and another reductive notion, that he is interested only in "content" and not in "form."

Meanwhile, in a chapter on Mei-Mei Berssenbrugge, whose work often appears in avant-garde poetry anthologies, Wang makes the case that even in poems that eschew logical narrative—using pronouns without antecedents, for instance, or deliberately mis-naming a place—and lack explicit references to race, the poet's situation in life should not be willfully ignored in understanding the poem. Surely a poet who was forced to switch languages because of migration would have special insight into the inadequacies of language to represent experience; Wang demonstrates this with several poems and adds emphasis with a statement on the subject from the poet. Yet Berssenbrugge's work is often praised in avant-garde circles for its omission of references to race or identity;

such references might pollute "form" with "content." Wang points out that the avant-garde poetry world is overwhelmingly white. She also makes the somewhat heartbreaking observation that by almost always making Berssenbrugge and Korean American poet Myung Mi Kim (whose work also tends to leave out racial markers) the Asian American poets in avant-garde anthologies, editors are able to have it both ways—to "pat themselves on the back for being open-minded enough to include people of color in their anthologies and readings" (247)—and to continue to avoid race.

Wang further solidifies her point by discussing Pamela Lu's *Pamela: A Novel* (1998), which is not a novel in any conventional sense, nor is it conventional as poetry or any other genre. Avoiding plot, dialogue, and character development, it depicts without specifically describing the lives of several young adults, whom the reader does and does not get to know. Like the poems of Berssenbrugge, *Pamela: A Novel* makes few overt references to race and has been called "avant-garde, post-racial, and post-identity" (297). Yet it is suffused with the consciousness of one who does not belong to the dominant group. Here is one example among several that Wang quotes:

> Often we felt tempted to page each other over the airport intercom system or to pick up the nearest White Courtesy Phone in response to any number of the muffled, unintelligible announcements that traveled over the airwaves of the intercom system, though R later pointed out, as soon as we were all reunited, that what we needed was not the White Courtesy Phone but rather the Other Courtesy Phone, a nonexistent piece of technology that would cater to the demands of our marginalized discourse and bring us together against the dominant paradigm of airport static and confusion (Lu 24-25).

At the same time, *Pamela: A Novel* questions the reality of perceived reality, the reality of the self, and the meaning and usefulness of representations such as maps and language. It explicitly calls out "those politicized art-forms that repeated clichés of 'displacement' and 'diaspora'" (Lu 18). But Wang points out that Lu's book does not posit that writing about racial identity is in itself a cliché. Rather, it suggests that all works about race are not the same. Some resort to tired formulae. Others are original, incisive, and necessary. Surely this is true of all books that share a theme or approach. Both Wang and Lu demonstrate that not all Asian American literary works that tangle with identity are the same, they are not categorically "bad," and there are many ways to approach the material.

This is the broadest and most oversimplified generalization one can take from *Thinking Its Presence*. It's unfortunate that such a statement needs such an extensive defense, but such is the world we live in. It is done rigorously in Wang's book, with the potential to open doors to different poets and schools of poetry, for readers of all persuasions.

2018

Art Is Long, Planets Short: The Lasting Power of Carol Ann Duffy's "The Woman in the Moon"

The Woman in the Moon

Darlings, I write to you from the moon
where I hide behind famous light.
How could you think it ever a man up here?
A cow jumped over. The dish ran away with

the spoon. What reached me were your joys, griefs,
here's-the-craic, losses, longings, your lives
brief, mine long, a talented loneliness. I must have
a thousand names for the earth, my blue vocation.

Round I go, the moon a diet of light, sliver of pear,
wedge of lemon, slice of melon, half an orange,
silver onion; your human sound falling through space,
childbirth's song, the lover's song, the song of death.

Devoted as words to things, I gaze, gawp, glare; deserts
where forests were, sick seas. When night comes,
I see you gaping back as though you hear my *Darlings,*
what have you done, what have you done to the world?

— Carol Ann Duffy

I HAVE MIXED feelings about my belief that Carol Ann Duffy's "The Woman in the Moon" is likely to endure well into and beyond the 21st century. The happy side is aesthetic: it has disciplined quatrains, playful alliteration, inconspicuous rhymes, and a cascade of clear images that are of the immortal kind. That metrical dexterity nods to centuries of poetic convention, and while free verse in English has been more popular than formal for some time now, contemporary poets of enduring power, like Duffy, readily deploy elements of unfree verse even when they are not writing in strict forms, in order to make poems as musically precise as they are creative and intellectual—the point of poetry. The reason I am unhappy that the poem is likely to be representative of this era is thematic. It's a piece about patriarchal power and the destruction of the planet, and its message is urgent.

"The Woman in the Moon" in the poem speaks in place of the archetypal "man in the moon," recasting that character as a woman who is irritated by the human assumption that this figure of legend must be male. In the wry voice of your most opinionated aunt (who always turns out to be right), she tells the inhabitants of Earth—addressed as "Darlings"—her thoughts on observing them through the ages. Affectionate and annoyed, she sympathizes with their struggles (*our* struggles) yet bemoans their abuse (*our* abuse) of the planet; and the poem's final sentence laments its destruction. On the way, the speaker shows herself to be a force not only of nurturing watchfulness but also of literary mastery. She is not talking but writing to us, it seems; and this woman in the moon is not just any writer. She is demonstrably a poet.

The first of the four quatrains establishes how underacknowledged she is, though: "I hide behind famous light." Like a woman poet obscured by more-reviewed, more-published male poets of her generation, the speaker occupies the same actual heights but remains unseen. As a figure of legend, she is similarly displaced. The exasperated third line, "How could you think it ever a man up here?", not only points to the moon's temporal connection to women, who unlike men are subject to monthly cycles, but also introduces familiar domestic images connected to the moon: "A cow jumped over. The dish ran away with / the spoon." The cow is domesticated, a source of milk; spoons and dishes feed people; and in their own way, those verses evoke childhood, early caregivers, and our first imaginings. While I would like to be able to counter my own remarks with the claim that the domestic is not necessarily feminine, women worldwide still spend significantly more time on unpaid domestic tasks than do their male counterparts, despite women's advances in the workplace. Duffy's woman in the moon seems to want us to consider that imbalance.

The language of stanza two remains maternal but quickly abandons nursery rhymes. While saying the verses, this mother-moon has not been thinking vacantly of cows and spoons but scrutinizing the experiences of her children down here on earth: "What reached me were your joys, griefs, / here's-the-craic, losses, longings..." The slangy "here's-the-craic" not only offers an embrace of Irishness ("craic" being Gaelic for "fun" or "a good time") by Britain's poet laureate, but it also brings familiarity to an otherwise general list. "Here's-the-craic" reflects the closeness of a daily caretaker, versus the distant concern of a guardian on high. Yet this guardian *is* on high. But she is still an intimate, and perhaps, the poem winks, the female moon-dweller has more knowledge of her charges than the male one, who's too busy soaking up notice to pay any mind to the daily details.

Duffy continues the list of human vicissitudes that reach up to the woman in the moon, but with a sleight-of-hand line break she turns our attention away from what this character might understand of us and toward our mortality: "What reached me were your joys, griefs, / here's-the-craic, losses, longings, your lives / brief, mine long, a talented loneliness." While "your lives" seems, at first, to be a part of what reaches the moon—this great listener—the line break suggests that those words are the beginning of a new idea. Instead of the connection between human lives and some outside force, then, we are reminded of our own smallness, briefness. The break also seems to show the speaker's reluctance to acknowledge that she will outlive her children, as well as a desire to shield those children from that reality for the brief interval during which she can hold it off.

Of course, that very break creates emphasis on "brief," and the word is an unwanted yet unavoidable shock. All our squabbles and craic are pretty insignificant, it seems, especially in relation to the moon, whose life is *not* brief. Immortality, under these circumstances, is overrated, causing "loneliness" for this moon, this poet, this woman. Yet it is also "a talented loneliness," a loneliness endowed with the skills to translate a pileup of our earthly losses into lines and stanzas. Indeed, the woman in the moon is undeniably lyrical in her understanding of us earth-dwellers, and the full sentence accumulates "s" and "l" sounds that amplify the losses and lonelinesses, yet with a soothing aural effect. It may be all slipping away, the poem suggests, but someone is straining to hear our call.

Still soft in sound, the "woman in the moon" then makes a surprising turn, as if stepping back for perspective, and estimates that she "must have / a thousand names for the earth, my blue vocation." That she has so many suggests that the earth itself, the environment, is another of her children, and subject to affectionate nicknames. For a moment, all those human lives become too numerous and microscopic to register individually. Meanwhile, the phrase "blue vocation" evokes the smallness of Earth seen from afar, and possible ambivalence toward her role as a watcher and empathizer (an ambivalence many mothers have likely felt). The job of overseeing us has become melancholic, and the woman in the moon, this listener, hears our Blues and sees our oceans as well, knowing our lives are often sad, and that Earth is under threat.

Tragic subject matter notwithstanding, Duffy's poem delights in language. Rhymes appear not at the traditional ends of lines but within. Four lines separate "moon" from "spoon"; "griefs" are echoed two lines later with "brief"; a "sliver of pear" is followed, also two lines later, by a "silver onion"; a catalog of foods to which the moon is compared includes "lemon," "melon," and "onion," invoking not only the harmony of those words pronounced in proximity but also the simple finery of the earth's products, in their elemental roundness.

These lines remind the reader to be grateful to have an onion to chop for dinner, "half an orange" to enjoy at breakfast, a "wedge of lemon" to squeeze into a cup of tea (although it is notable that we mostly see slices, not whole fruits, as if the bounty were not altogether satisfying, or being shared equally). While the rhymes are not obvious to the eye, they echo in the ear, and the poem's organized affirmation of rhyme combined with the rejection of its traditional positioning suggests that our received notions of form—like the old pattern of the seasons, now thrown off by climate change—are being upended. Yet all is not lost; art can still make rhythms, beauty, pleasure, and order.

Those mellifluous-sounding foods, which make up half of Duffy's third stanza, not only illustrate the moon's appearance but also reflect what the speaker has to eat. There is no mention of green cheese. Rather, lunar life resembles a feminine, fat-free lunch: "Round I go, the moon a diet of light, sliver of pear, / wedge of lemon, slice of melon, half an orange, / silver onion," the word "diet" preceding what sounds like a peculiar fruit salad, starting with the zero-calorie "light." The adjacent orbiting—"Round I go"—even hints at an effort to stay fit (and, of course, slender) on an elliptical machine, stationary bicycle, or track. But just as she does not fully inhabit a nursery rhyme at the outset, nor is the speaker listening to mindless workout music. Instead, our heroine tunes in to "your human sound falling through space, / childbirth's song, the lover's song, the song of death": the woman in the moon, a consummate poet, listens to life in all its grandeur, its joys and tragedies.

In addition to her literary obscurity, the speaker shares with many human mothers the condition of being undervalued in her work, as her tireless vigilance seems to be taken for granted. Yet the poem's humans know that *someone* is watching; at night, in the final stanza, the speaker notices people staring up at her, "gaping back as though [they] hear," as they search the sky for forces greater than themselves. Unsaid but implicit is the baselessness of their assumption that God (along with the equivalent of God in most religions) takes masculine form. Meanwhile, the phrase "as though you hear" does double duty: not only can people not hear "the woman in the moon" because she is hidden and far away, they also cannot or will not hear warnings about global warming, no matter how audible, fact-based, or accessible.

Part of what makes the poem contemporary but certain to last is that it does not dwell on the ongoing destruction of the planet but takes it as a fait accompli, which will seem natural to a future reader of the early 21st century canon. Its final cry—"*Darlings, / what have you done, what have you done to the world?*"—echoes a mother finding her children with a broken vase, perhaps an inher- ited, irreplaceable one. The poem does not overtly urge readers to help save the planet but grieves over its degradation. This grief functions rhetorically now (if indeed the planet is still salvageable) as an exhortation to action, but it also applies literally to the day we seem to be hurtling toward, when the planet has been irrevers- ibly ruined. That is, the poem works one way now and will work another way later.

The alarm about the earth becomes clear in the sound as the poem lulls and then surprises us with jarring rhythms. After the nearly iambic "childbirth's song, the lover's song, the song of death. / Devoted as words to things," the speaker looks upon destruction with three consecutive stressed (and alliterative) syllables: "I gaze, gawp, glare," seeing not only "deserts / where forests were" but also the spondaic "sick seas." The closing lament—"*what you have done, what have you done*"—receives emphasis from the stress on "what" and "done" twice over. Meanwhile, the speaker invokes language as a fellow protector—she calls herself "Devoted as words to things"—as if to suggest that words, despite their parallel inability to save the planet or even name its components accurately, are an alternate form of salvation. In Carol Ann Duffy's "The Woman in the Moon," language and listening may be imperfect and may not connect us. But the speaker seems to believe that if earth is careening toward ruin, its inhabitants might as well go singing.

2018

· 4 ·

Sustenance, Culinary and Literary

A Sense of Home: Notes on
Section Four

MANY WRITERS, asked about their motivation for writing a particular book, respond that they wrote the book they wanted to read. While I might not give that exact answer on behalf of this collection, which accrued over decades, the drive to keep it going was related: I have always been in search of literary works that combine my passions for poetry and for cooking. That combination alone has been rare enough; to hope for an Asian American dimension—never mind a Southern one—seemed to guarantee frustration.

But conditions change over time. Asian American writers, including Southern ones, are no longer hard to find. Writings on Southern food are often forward-looking and imaginative rather than mired in nostalgia. Food is no longer a marginal topic among poets, so this section's first five pieces—on food and poets but in one instance on food alone—first entered the world on *The Best American Poetry* blog. The two long pieces that follow them examine Chinese Americanness through children's books ("You Are What You Read") and Chinese restaurants in America ("Between the Shopping Cart and the Chinese Restaurant"). Reading and eating may seem to be separate (though they can often be done simultaneously), but for many—cookbook readers, Food Studies students, anyone who wants to contemplate the ethics of how they feed their minds and bodies—these two elemental activities collide in meaningful ways.

"North and South," which I wrote quickly in response to a horrific crime, is not centrally about food, but food is one of the metaphors by which I attempt to understand events that defy understanding.

The Pauses between Poems

MOST OF the poets I know have been temporarily silenced, at least in verse, by the COVID-19 crisis. Recent months recall the aftermaths of 9/11 and the 2016 presidential election: impossible to write creatively about, impossible to turn away from. To seek the distance needed to transform experience into reflection feels like closing your eyes at the wheel. To wander into gray areas, so that a poem might begin in one place and end in another, requires a surrounding prevalence of non-gray areas. Now everything is gray, and wandering hazardous.

Was it really only a short time ago that the average poet was maneuvering to maximize writing time, stealing half an hour before a work meeting, setting alarms fifteen, then twenty minutes earlier than normal, or making notes in a parked car or real-life waiting room? As recently as February, when poem-making conditions were normal, I was identifying strategies for increasing writing time by reducing time spent planning, shopping for, and preparing meals, without giving in to joyless repetition, frozen dinners, or excess takeout.

I'm more of an authority on the latter (not giving in) than the former (kitchen shortcuts), although I'm interested in both. Even before the rituals of eating became central to life under lockdown, I saw every meal as a chance to celebrate being alive and able to savor breakfast, lunch, dinner, or one of the many semi-meals I sneak in between. It's a near-obsession. Despite repeated culling and frequent visits to the library, I have nearly 300 cookbooks, in addition to several shelves of food nonfiction. Over the years, including many spent parenting alone, I've assembled an army of appliances meant to save time—pressure cooker, stand mixer, food processor, programmable rice cooker, immersion blender, Vitamix—but also a number of things that aren't about saving time: canning supplies, ice-cream maker, pizza stone, cake-decorating tools, and an admittedly neglected manual pasta machine. When there's room for it, cooking is a pleasure and the closest thing I have to a hobby. Yet I find (or, pre-pandemic, found) myself constantly chafing at having to choose between writing and cooking, and resenting cooking for so being relentlessly non-optional.

Before the novel coronavirus upended routines, I often got up early Sunday, intending to go to the grocery store while everyone else was either at church (this is rural Pennsylvania) or lingering over waffles. I'd list what ingredients needed to be used up, then create a week's worth of menus that called for them, thus generating a second list, of what to buy. But I tend to page through cookbooks as if they were restaurant menus: "I'll have the pesto-grilled salmon, please, with butternut-squash risotto and a side of broccoli rabe, probably followed by peach cobbler with vanilla ice cream," with the intention, the next day, of switching to Chinese food. The list would grow complicated, requiring stops at multiple stores. By the time I actually reached the first store, it was crowded, and by the time I finished shopping, it was mid-afternoon. If I wanted to make lunches to take to work that week *and* dinner for that night, I'd have to start cooking right away. What happened to my plan to shop early, then have a little bit of Sunday to write?

Somehow, over time, though, the writing got done. That most of it has recently been about food is relevant, but domestic chores can be the enemy of writing about anything, including domestic chores. I've unwittingly cut other things out—I've missed out on most movies, for instance—but, stepping back now, realize that I'm not completely inefficient in the kitchen. Over time I've developed a few ways to nourish a day of writing, on the occasion that such a rare day can be found, without too much compromise on taste. This week I'll talk about some of these strategies, with input from a few other poets on sustenance and writing (or sustenance and lockdown).

In the meantime, I say to any poet who can't write poems these days, I'm with you. I can't, either, especially as each day's bad news keeps multiplying in scale and range. But not writing poems isn't bothering me yet. From a writing point of view, I've found the COVID-19 crisis to be, in addition to a mass tragedy and magnification of inequality, a reminder that silences are nothing new. I didn't write in the immediate aftermath of childbirth, or in the time around any move, or while starting my teaching career. I've even had days of silence in an artists' colony, which in pragmatic terms is a waste but in creative terms, natural. Writing is a conversation. Sometimes you talk, other times you listen, and what you eventually say is more meaningful for your having listened. The entity you're conversing with might not care what you think—it may even want to do you mortal harm—but by listening to it (while doing everything you can to avoid infection by it), you are developing a response. Like the vaccine we're all waiting for, that response could take a long time. Pandemic-prompted non-writing can be a form of writing. By paying attention, we shape the white space around our lines and stanzas. That white space is not the absence of poem but a defining element of a poem's structure. In the meantime, whether or not we're able to compose a line, we have to eat.

A Bright Green Side of Broccoli Rabe

1 bunch broccoli rabe, about 1 lb.
1 Tbsp. extra-virgin olive oil
2 cloves garlic, peeled and coarsely chopped
Salt
¼ tsp. crushed red pepper flakes or a seasoning blend
    such as Penzeys Tuscan Sunset, Florida Seasoned Pepper,
    or Lemon Pepper

1. Put a large pot of water on to boil, as if you were cooking pasta, over high heat. (If you *are* cooking pasta, reserve the hot water for it in step 3.)

2. While the water heats, rinse the broccoli rabe, then cut the small stems and florets into 2-inch lengths. Using a paring knife, peel the outer layer of skin from the thick stems, then cut them into 1-inch lengths. As you cut, collect the thick stems in one bowl, the leafy florets and small stems together in another.

3. When the water comes to a boil, add a tablespoon or so of salt. Then add the thicker stems of the broccoli rabe. A minute later, add the florets and small stems. Stir briefly, let the water return to a boil, then drain the rabe and spray with cold water to arrest its vibrant color. Drain well. At this point, you can set it aside until close to serving time, even refrigerate it overnight.

4. Shortly before you're ready to eat, heat the olive oil in a wide saucepan (12" is nice) over medium heat. Add the garlic and stir until it's fragrant but not browned, a few seconds. Add the drained broccoli rabe, stir to coat with the

garlicky oil, and season with red pepper flakes or seasoning blend and salt to taste. Toss and stir until heated through, a couple of minutes, adding an extra minute or so if the greens were refrigerated.

About 4 servings, 2 if you love bitter greens

2020

WITHOUT RESTAURANTS

POET FAITH SHEARIN reports from sheltering-in-place in Massachusetts:

We are cooking a ton because even the carry-out in Amherst and Northampton has shut down. I miss restaurants more than I can say. I love a lot of food I don't know how to cook: Indian, Thai, Chinese, Japanese, Vietnamese... Our COVID diet consists largely of the things I was raised on. Several generations of my ancestors drank iced tea and ate fried chicken in eastern North Carolina; I made my first batch of cornbread with my great grandmother before I learned to read. My great grandparents were farmers and corn was their most prolific crop. I was served grits with one soppy egg for breakfast, and cornbread with most soups; both sides of my family were devoted to Brunswick Stew. Nobody could completely agree about the ingredients in this dish so a lot was left to interpretation and imagination. I like to pull the chicken off a freshly cooked bird, dice some onions and garlic, chop basil, then add corn, red potatoes, and lima beans to a broth that is half tomato sauce half chicken broth. One grandmother liked to add green beans; another favored several meats, including pork. Some

folks make it thin, with tomato juice, and some make it
thicker with tomato paste. I make cornbread like this: 2
and 1/2 cups of coarse ground cornmeal, 1/2 teaspoon
baking soda, 1/2 teaspoon salt, 1 egg, 1 and 1/3 cup buttermilk, 2 tablespoons of butter. Cook at 375 for 25 minutes. I sometimes serve the stew with a spinach salad
or make a fruit cobbler to go with it, or I throw a sweet
potato in the oven and serve it with a little bit of butter
and brown sugar. I like to cook when I am in the mood
and rapidly tire of it when I'm doing it three times a day.
I know a lot of people feel like this. The food I can cook
well is the food I learned to make from my grandparents;
it tastes like childhood.

Faith and I are old friends. We both call the American South
home—Kitty Hawk, NC, for Faith; Atlanta, GA, for me—but both
live now in places where cornbread and Brunswick stew are more
novelties than staples. Although my family arrived in the South
much later than Faith's did and our fried chicken was more likely to
come from a restaurant than a cast-iron skillet on the stove, I share
her connection to fruit cobbler and grits, and felt the estrangement
when I first moved North. My Thanksgiving stuffing is cornbread-
based. Like Faith, I cherish Indian, Chinese, Thai, Japanese, and
Vietnamese restaurants. My grandmothers cooked Chinese food,
but I didn't grow up cooking with my grandmothers, as the link had
been broken by World War II and the Chinese Communist revolution; I never met my paternal grandmother. My mother, driven
with her family from their home in Shanghai when she was a child,
had to teach herself how to cook Chinese food in 1960s Atlanta,
which meant the ingredients were Southern-inflected, the techniques explained in English by Joyce Chen and Grace Zia Chu. But
because she knew how the dishes were supposed to look and taste,
my mother was well-prepared to use (and adapt) the instructions.

By the mid-1980s, Atlanta's Chinese restaurants had multiplied approximately one hundredfold since my father's arrival in 1948; many catered to a Chinese clientele. Our lives had reached the point where time was scarcer than money, so we often lived on good-quality takeout plus home-cooked rice and vegetables.

Faith's lockdown-narrowed diet reminds me that the foods we associate with comfort and home are not necessarily made in the home. Restaurants build meaningful family memory, too. In the absence of restaurants, her longing for, say, tofu with bok choy is no less a part of who she is than her skill in turning out a Brunswick stew; it only joined the family later. This spell of eating what we can without restaurants is an opportunity to expand self-knowledge. What do we miss the most, and what is different about us without it? What skills from previous generations—even if we have to imagine them, as I imagine Faith's great grandparents in a bad year for corn, or each of my parents as a foreign student in Georgia, faced with the mystery of buttermilk or white gravy—are we calling on now? What do we know how to cook that, out of forgetfulness or the excitement of the new, we haven't cooked in a decade and are bringing back because the pantry, or a pandemic-driven sense of continuity with lost forebears, points to it? It's worth recording, occasionally if not regularly, what we're eating these days, as well as what we aren't. One day we'll be able to look at the list, understand what it reveals, and possibly even write again, with new perspective on who we've become.

2020

Everything in Its Place

P OET AND MEMOIRIST Sandra Beasley cooks differently depending on whether she's writing poetry or prose:

> I'm a tremendous fan of *mise en place*; one of my favorite wedding gifts was a stack of glass nesting bowls that I use. I'm methodical, which, to be honest, is something that I pride myself on as a poet as well... For prose, I'm a mess—indulgent snacking, weird sleep and meal hours, hoping my husband does most of the cooking! I get overwhelmed with the scale of prose projects. I cook better as a poet.

I can't help but connect this to Sandra's facility with forms. Writing a sonnet or sestina is an overt act of ordering raw material, taking the chaos of human existence and working it into a recognizable shape, with strict rules governing what can appear at the end of each line, how many lines there will be, and sometimes how many stresses each line should contain. Many good formal poems break some of the rules, within the bounds of what I call, in the classroom, not looking like a mistake. One could argue that free-verse poems do the same—give shape to the shapelessness of experience—and the best free verse does exactly that. But something about *mise en place* mirrors the compulsive neatness of rhymed quatrains, the symmetry of a pantoum returning to its first and third lines as it completes its mission of saying every line twice, without ever quite repeating itself.

A fellow devotee of forms, I've made similar efforts to create order in the kitchen. I share Sandra's enthusiasm for *mise en place*, which is essential for the speed of Chinese cooking (the actual cooking, not the prep, being speedy). I also do—or did, pre-COVID— methodical lunch preparation. Ideally, I'd start the work week with a stockpile of homemade lunches. Worth the effort: a makeshift sardine banh mi, the carrots and radishes quick-pickled; calamari and white bean salad, with mesclun or farro in the other compart- ment; a bowl (as in grain, protein, vegetable, pickles). It isn't quick, but making several at once cuts down the time spent per lunch. Seeing the containers stacked in the fridge erases a daily problem from the week and pre-empts the junky snacking that follows a hastily purchased, not-really-what-you-wanted sandwich. Most of all, *thinking* about lunch is over until the weekend.

Some advance-lunch guidelines: Once you have your stash, don't give in to the temptation to eat one for dinner midweek; not only will you lose a day, you'll also get tired of it. Don't repeat a lunch for two consecutive weeks; you'll get tired of it. Sauce or dressing should travel in its own container, to be mixed just before you eat. If the lunch involves good bread, slice and freeze the bread for the week, thawing what you need for the next day overnight, or let it thaw in your lunch bag during the morning. Some ingredients have to be added the day you eat, such as avocado; use a reminder app to carry the mental load of remembering to add them. Keep salt and pepper at work. If you have the space where you work and it's allowed, having a small toaster oven there can be life-changing.

It's hard to fend off the notion that poetry writing is an irrational, struck-by-lightning activity that doesn't respond to ongoing effort. For sure, there are days when it seems to resist. But writing of any kind works better when you keep trying, and it's less intimidating if you view writing as a form of organizing. Sandra reports about cooking systematically: "I use that cooking time for planning writing projects; in this case, I was working toward delivering a commissioned poem on deadline." I find this reassuring evidence that poems are made, not granted by deities. And on those days when kitchen organization seems impossible and you keep reaching for the chips, maybe that's a good time to muck around in a larger, more sprawling project, dare I say prose?

2020

THE TWO KINDS OF POETS

I HAVE AN informal, untested theory that when it comes to sustenance while writing, there are two kinds of poets: coffee poets and food poets. Coffee poets (who in some cases could be considered tea poets) can go half the day or longer without solid food; their focus is sustainable without the distraction and mess of eating. Coffee poets who are also capable of writing in public spaces are doubly blessed, as they can log many hours in a cafe without having to incur the expense of meals with their beverages, or the interruption of leaving for lunch. Bringing a thermos, they can bide their time in libraries, getting lost in the books they're reading and writing, enjoying a communal version of a solitary activity.

As a food poet, one whose energy levels are better maintained by six small meals a day versus three large, I envy coffee poets their long stretches of concentration. They aren't constantly reminded by hunger of their profane, alimentary existence as human animals. When they write at home, their kitchen sinks don't fill with dishes within the first three hours. Their keyboards don't get sticky or greasy. They don't end a day of writing only to realize that, bit by bit, they have eaten all of last night's leftovers and there is nothing for dinner.

The inimitable Kazim Ali is a coffee poet:

Early morning is my writing time—and coffee is the key
to my experience. I buy beans from local roasters, preferably organic. My favorite is Mexican coffee, the darker
the roast the better. I used to hand grind the beans (more
for the meditation quality of doing the work, rather than
any notion of coffee purity) but now I just have a little
grinder for them. In the past I swore by the French press
or a pour-over if I was only drinking a cup, but these days
I make drip coffee in a coffee-maker because it's easier
to make a lot and keep it hot. If I don't drink it black, I'll
drink it with stevia and almond or oat milk. Mahmoud
Darwish (in that rapturous extended passage near the
beginning of his memoir of the Beirut bombing of 1982)
says "Coffee is the sister of time," and I believe it. I hover
over sentences with that warm company.

Kazim, who in addition to poetry has written memoir, criticism,
novels, and translations, while also building a distinguished record
of editing and teaching, is clearly driven by more than coffee. Yet
knowing this detail about his process suggests that we food poets
might do well to streamline the way we work, to be more like coffee
poets, only with food. We can't cut food-preparation time down to
that of brewing coffee, but we can aspire to limit it on certain days.

Generally, when cooking, I find that I have to be all in, mindfully
trimming fat, fishing out lemon seeds with a tiny measuring spoon,
intuiting the springiness of dough. Otherwise, I cut or burn myself,
or over- or undercook things. Most "quick and easy" recipes don't
work for me; they spur an inattention that ends in disappointment.
Yet on the rare occasion that I find myself free to write for a day
or the better part of a day, I don't want to dwell in cooking. I also
don't want to resort to a giant pot of stew that has to be eaten so
many times that you never want to see it again, the way dogs resign
themselves to their kibble after begging for what you're having.

Here are a few ways to hang back from the kingdom of cooking while trying to sidestep taste fatigue:

- Embrace the powers of the microwave, which generates less dishwashing than conventional cooking and in summer keeps the kitchen cool. I've been making the Szechuan Green Beans in Barbara Kafka's *Microwave Gourmet* for decades; it cooks in the dish it's served in. (Barbara Kafka started out as a poet.) Marie T. Smith's memorably titled *Microwave Cooking for One* helped me finish my last book; the chili and the fish chowder are as simple and good as promised, and the recipes multiply for when you're not isolating. Julie Sahni's *Moghul Microwave* contains miracles, too, among them Parsi Chicken and Savory Keema Cake.

- Cook extra of whatever you're making the day before, but make sure it includes two or more of these elements: spicy, sour, bitter, fermented, or contrasting textures. Having to eat the same dish over and over is more tolerable when it has complexity; it takes me a long time to tire of Chinese spicy noodles, in vegetarian or carnivorous versions, hot or cold, inflected with some or all of these: sesame paste, peanut butter, black vinegar, chili oil, a touch of sweetness.

- Cook extra dinner before your writing day, but with specific plans to transform the leftovers into something different. Two books that can help with this are *Leftovers* by Kathy Gunst and *Green Plate Special* by Christine Rudalevige.

- Do what my parents did when raising teenagers and working: order rice-based takeout meals, then extend them with your own rice and vegetables, keeping the vegetables easy: sliced

Napa cabbage simmered in chicken broth, stir-fried broccoli
or asparagus.

- Team up with a local "food poet" friend whose eating prefer-
  ences are compatible with yours, even if lockdown forbids
  eating together. Each of you cooks a dish, then gives half to
  the other.

Chances are, you will still spend more time in the kitchen than a
coffee poet will. But channel Kazim's observation about the "meditation quality of doing the work," and adapt the wisdom of Mahmoud Darwish to your own temperament. Spicy noodles, too, can
be the sister of time.

2020

Two Dozen Reasons to Make Dinner

Twelve Ways Cooking Is Empowering:

1. When you look into the refrigerator at what used to elicit a wail of "there's nothing to eat," you see the makings of a frittata, pizza, or fried rice.
2. After making and eating the frittata, pizza, or fried rice, you can gloat about not having wasted the scraps in the refrigerator.
3. Scraps in the refrigerator start to look less like clutter and more like material for a creative project.
4. If you're working on a creative project unlikely to generate income, such as a book of poems, you can turn humble ingredients into excellent food.
5. What's in your food is under your control.
6. You can't always control how a dish will turn out, but you can learn from disappointments.
7. Even with occasional disappointments, your house smells terrific and feels like a home.
8. After cooking, you're forced to clean your house, or at least the kitchen, thus supporting another round of cooking.
9. You can directly support people who are sick, mourning, occupied with a new baby, protesting, or simply living their lives.

10. If you live in a place where restaurants don't serve what you long for, you can still have many of the dishes you crave.
11. You have fewer cravings for sweets and snacks because you don't feel, after a meal, that something is missing.
12. Fewer things are missing.

Twelve Usable Cookbooks:

1. America's Test Kitchen, *Bowls*
2. Irene Kuo, *The Key to Chinese Cooking*
3. Florence Lin, *Florence Lin's Chinese Regional Cookbook*
4. Deborah Madison, *Vegetarian Cooking for Everyone*
5. Peter Meehan et al, *Lucky Peach Presents 100 Easy Asian Recipes*
6. Urvashi Pitre, *Indian Instant Pot Cookbook*
7. Susan Purdy, *The Family Baker*
8. Julie Sahni, *Classic Indian Cooking*
9. Lorna Sass, *Whole Grains Every Day, Every Way*
10. Ellen Schrecker, *Mrs. Chiang's Szechwan Cookbook*
11. Alice Waters, *The Art of Simple Food*
12. Diana Henry, *From the Oven to the Table*

2020

You Are What You Read

S INCE MY PARENTS always made room for more books in our
Atlanta home, I thought I knew what I was doing when, at six,
I decided to be a writer. I wrote my first "poem" soon afterwards,
in 1974, and never went back on the decision, producing stories,
poems, and attempts at novels. Yet not until college did I write from
the perspective of an Asian American speaker. One reason for the
delay is surely that children's books with Asian, never mind Asian
American, characters were vanishingly scarce. A 2016 study by
Angela Christine Moffett, "Exploring Racial Diversity in Caldecott
Medal-Winning and Honor Books," found that of the 332 Caldecott
books published between 1939 and 2016, thirteen, or 1%, had Asian
or Asian American primary characters. My brother and I recall
from our childhood only two picture books with Asian main characters, *The Five Chinese Brothers* by Claire Huchet Bishop and illustrated by Kurt Wiese (1938) and *Tikki Tikki Tembo* by Arlene Mosel
and illustrated by Blair Lent (1968), both of which are still in print.

The Five Chinese Brothers, in which the titular characters use
superpowers to evade a death sentence, has been criticized for
racially caricatured illustrations and the unexplained identicalness
of the brothers. Defenders argue that the book evokes nostalgia for
many, the art represents a different time, and it's based on a Chinese folktale.

I understand the nostalgia, having enjoyed the book in childhood. I had never been to China, so for all I knew, it was accurate: men wearing queues, justice by beheading, identical (non-quintuplet) siblings, secret superpowers. But nostalgia doesn't preclude adult awareness of a book's shortcomings and young children's inability to apply historical perspective. My own children, now in high school and college, didn't encounter *The Five Chinese Brothers* until this year. They were appalled, in part because they are capable, as they were not as three-year-olds, of recognizing racial stereotypes, in part because the books they read as young children, while still lacking in main characters of Asian descent, had more than the books of my generation did, and included Asian American characters. On our shelves were *Into My Mother's Arms* by Sharon Jennings, illustrated by Ruth Ohi; *Yoko* by Rosemary Wells; and *Lon Po Po* by Ed Young (although the anti-wolf angle didn't sit well). The board book *More More More, Said the Baby* by Vera B. Williams includes an Asian baby. Though we didn't have Amy Tan's *Sagwa* book, we had the DVDs. These represented an improvement over my era in more than quantity. While *Sagwa* is set in a China of flowing robes and sleeve-dwelling toy dogs, its characters have the normal flaws that make for good storytelling. *Yoko,* using animal characters, features a Japanese American girl who is mocked for bringing sushi to school, a literary scene that would have made a difference for me at picture-book age. In the Jennings and Williams books, being of Asian descent is an inherent part of life and not a subject of commentary.

On the whole, however, my kids' early reading, three decades after mine, was dominated by white characters. Well-worn books in our house included Laura Numeroff's *If You Give a Mouse a Cookie* series, Susan Meddaugh's *Martha Speaks,* Mark Teague's *Dear Mrs. LaRue,* and many picture books by Jan Brett. Others were hand-me-downs (perhaps a cousin of nostalgia picks) or simply canonized: *Make Way for Ducklings* by Robert McCloskey, *Madeline* by Ludwig Bemelmans, *Curious George,* and much of Dr. Seuss.

While it could be based on a Chinese folktale, the narration of *The Five Chinese Brothers* does not reflect a Chinese perspective. The story is set in China, yet the brothers are always referred to as "the first Chinese brother," "the second Chinese brother," etc., while other characters are "the little boy," "the judge," "the executioner." That is, the adjective distinguishing characters with superpowers from normal ones is not "Wonder" or "Super" but the redundant "Chinese." The brothers' imperviousness to decapitation, drowning, fire, and suffocation also encourages the notion that a "Chinese" person does not feel pain.

As a child reading it, I was too young to realize that neighbors, using the same libraries, might perceive my family through the lens of the book. Asians were so few in Atlanta that if I went somewhere with an Asian American friend, people assumed we were related. On occasion we made it a joke and spoke gibberish to each other to make them think we were speaking Chinese (or Japanese or Korean—whatever they thought we were). One class in high school held a spontaneous discussion of how to tell the two East Asian girls in the class apart, commenting on the few physical features they thought might be used to do so, while the two of us sat in mortified silence. That our classmates may have had only *The Five Chinese Brothers* as an early depiction of Asianness didn't help, since the brothers "all looked exactly alike." Asian kids—mainly of Chinese descent in my schools—were also regarded as academic achievers, the "model minority," which, like superpowers, looks positive on its surface, but its effect was to prevent Asian-Black solidarity. It was also misleading. Most of the Chinese American kids I knew had highly educated parents who had arrived before the Immigration and Nationality Act (1965) inadvertently relaxed longstanding U.S. restrictions on immigration from Asia. The reason so many of our fathers had PhDs in engineering and the sciences, and so many of our mothers were college-educated, some with advanced degrees as well, was not a genetic predisposition but U.S.

immigration policy. A Cold War effort to keep technical expertise in the U.S. rather than exporting it to communist China resulted in these exceptions to the official cap of 105 Chinese immigrants per year. So, many students and established experts in science and engineering—some of whom had been actively sought from Hong Kong and Taiwan by the U.S., and some of whom had been rendered stateless by the 1949 communist takeover of mainland China—stayed.

While Claire Huchet Bishop probably meant only to bring an enjoyable Chinese tale to American children in the 1930s, English-language authors retelling Chinese legends (and others stocking library shelves or compiling reading lists) might consider context: What in China would be one among hundreds of stories risks becoming the dominant "Chinese" narrative in U.S. children's literature in 1938, and even 1970. One pernicious assumption may be that the percentage of literary characters of a race need only match the percentage of the population to be sufficient. But that ignores the consequences of having only a handful of narratives for each underrepresented group. Not only does it harm the members of the group by creating what Chimamanda Ngozi Adichie, in a TED talk, calls "the danger of a single story," it also promotes narrowness of thinking among the general population. Some politicians may consider narrow thinking desirable for pragmatic reasons, but it's probably not the goal of teachers and librarians.

Tikki Tikki Tembo, in which a family learns not to favor one child over another, is less exoticizing than *Brothers* but also presents difficulties. The art shows "Chinese" people whose garb resembles Japanese geta and kimonos. The favored child's long name is nonsense, his brother's short name, Chang, mistranslated. Children's book author Grace Lin, on her blog, debunks the book's claims that Chinese families used to give favored sons long names and that the story is a Chinese folktale; more likely, it's an adaptation of a Japanese one. Acknowledging the affection many parents and teachers have for the tale, Lin suggests telling the story without the book, situating it in an unnamed land, and changing Chang's name so as not to point to China—or presenting the book alongside a discussion of truth vs. fiction, along with other books that accurately depict China.

I was given no such context, so the book's conflations were lost on me. I loved the moral satisfaction of the ending and recited the name "Tikki tikki tembo-no sa rembo-chari bari ruchi-pip peri pembo" for fun but now realize that it fed the "ching-chong" taunts all Asian Americans endure. When an Asian American friend and I spoke rubbish on purpose in public, we were unwittingly feeding those taunts. In addition, I was too young to perceive that, in a landscape lacking in counternarratives, *Tikki Tikki Tembo* encouraged the image of Chinese people as holders of ancient wisdom— another stereotype that appears positive but in isolation keeps them from being perceived as normal human beings. As a child, I never encountered in a book an Asian American kid who has ordinary experiences, such as friendship trouble or a neighborhood mystery to be solved. It would have been life-changing, when I was a little older, for one of Nancy Drew's friends to be Asian American. (Even today, my vision of a retroactively improved young people's literature assigns Asian descent not to the main character but to one of her sidekicks.) The handful of Asian characters I *did* meet were foreign. They were also mythical, embedded in a distant past, or both: in a word, exotic.

I recall two other early "Asian" literary encounters. One would be lost if the Dr. Seuss estate hadn't reminded me: the offending pages in, among other books, *If I Ran the Zoo* (1950), which I was too young to critique (its Asian characters are "helpers who all wear their eyes at a slant"). The other occurred a few years later. I loved the *Holidays and Customs* volume of the Childcraft encyclopedia until I opened it to a photo of an Asian child eating, under the headline "Eating with Sticks?"

As a book-loving child who admired encyclopedias as though they were books to the tenth power, I felt punched. Chopsticks as tools of crude stabbing? By then I could picture the author picturing the reader, and that default reader has never seen chopsticks.

I knew that most kids at school didn't know how to use chopsticks, but those who came to my house and opted for a fork knew what chopsticks were—and our silverware drawer had everything at the ready: forks, knives, Western-style spoons, Chinese-style spoons, and chopsticks. To my family, there was nothing alien about eating with a fork and knife; there were simply some tasks for which chopsticks were better (including safely extracting a stuck piece of toast from the toaster). What the Childcraft headline did was create for me the possibility that most of our neighbors, even those who came over and were too polite to express it, might be secretly aghast at the savagery of our utensils. "Eating with Sticks?" caused me to imagine them imagining us, which became a source of long-term fascination, as well as a provocation to write poems.

In retrospect, I see plenty of examples of China imagined by the West in my early surroundings. Sometimes it functioned as an immigrant tool of survival. Chinese restaurants, needing to attract a clientele that knew little of Chinese cooking, offered accessible Oriental adventure: animal-zodiac placemats, bright red booths, enormous dragons, fortune cookies (not of Chinese origin), and dramatic presentation (sizzling rice soup with its crackling rice, the pu pu platter with flames leaping out of a miniature grill). One of my aunts ran an "Oriental gift shop" in New Jersey. I loved visiting her store and helping to arrange the trinkets, often wanting to buy them (she usually gave them to me; I was probably not much of a helper). Since this was long before everyone could cheaply and easily order Chinese products, the store did well, surely bolstered by popular notions of the mysterious East. In elementary school, I did a social-studies project about silk, mainly because my mother had swatches on hand. Whether she had them because we were Chinese or because she was an excellent seamstress, I had no idea, but presenting them on the trifold board gave my project a look of authority—dare I say authenticity?—that made me think I must be Chinese, because everyone around me thought I was.

One refreshing moment of contrast was the 1970s TV commercial for the water softener Calgon, in which a Chinese American laundry owner, talking to a white customer, claims an "ancient Chinese secret" to getting clothes clean; his wife, also Chinese American, scoffs and reveals the true secret, Calgon. In an era when Asian Americans almost never appeared on TV, the ad is surprising for its readiness to poke fun at stereotypes and show Chinese Americans doing that all-American thing: running a small business, even if that business was a laundry, which was never a Chinese specialty but one of the few forms of work available to Chinese men in Gold Rush California. (Chinese women were largely barred from immigrating.) White resentment had driven them out of the mines, and the overall scarcity of women in the region had created demand for feminized labor, which is also how Chinese restaurants took hold in the American landscape: most men with other options refused to cook or wash clothes for a living. Opening a laundry, though physically taxing at the time, also enabled Chinese men, who faced overt racial discrimination in the labor market, to be self-employed.

The word "authentic" would hound me as an adult, especially after I developed an interest in the literature of food. Along with "ethnic," it has become a troubled word in the food world, linked to the pigeonholing of nonwhite chefs, who have long been judged on their ability to reproduce a rigid repertoire of "classic" dishes of their ancestral countries, even if they would prefer to innovate. This situation was not created by any individual book, but a paucity of early narratives primes the public mind to associate certain groups with idealized lands that tend toward the "far, far away" and "long, long ago," a habit that, unquestioned, can last a lifetime and be handed down. Every person, like every cuisine, is equally possessed of ethnicity; ethnicity is simply less obvious in members of the dominant group in a given place. "Authenticity" in popular usage freezes cuisines the world over into fixed, arbitrary notions of a culture's essence, when in fact the global exchange of ingredients and techniques has been happening for centuries; the potato's journey from Peru to Ireland is one of many examples. (I love the badge on the back cover of Lucky Peach's 2015 book *101 Easy Asian Recipes:* "100% Inauthentic!") In college I would find myself studying Chinese language, history, philosophy, and religion, all through texts written in English, which were further examples of the West imagining China. I would go to China as a foreign exchange student and discover how very Chinese I was not—that while my life had Chinese dimensions, I too had been, all along, another Westerner imagining China.

All of that was still in the future. As the 1980s approached and Chinese restaurants in Atlanta grew more numerous, I heard the word "authentic" used to distinguish restaurants that appealed mainly to Chinese palates from those that catered to mainstream American tastes—the Chinese restaurants of my early childhood. I'm sure I used it that way, too, and many still do, with benign intentions. It has utility in contexts where "Chinese" is neatly separated from "American." But in a nation that has had Chinese restaurants since the Gold Rush, the notion that the food served in these restaurants can be "authentic" only insofar as it reproduces Chinese tradition, rather than being accepted as a legitimate, dare I say "authentic," American food looks peculiar, especially when considering another immigrant food that was viewed as strange upon arrival, also in the mid-to-late nineteenth century: pizza.

The moment when I opened the children's encyclopedia to "Eating with Sticks?" stuck with me for decades. It generated a poem I published in *Prairie Schooner* in 1996, "Visions of Rice," which shows that episode returning to haunt me some twenty years later. In the poem, I have left the suburban South and set up house in "New York City, where the sophisticated people know how to eat with sticks," but still have flashbacks to that day; even in adulthood, the same chill descends and the rice of my childhood turns alien, even grotesque, despite its central place on my grown-up table and broad acceptance by urban elites. The poem is in none of my books. Chronologically, it should be in the first, *Middle Kingdom* (1997). I probably cut it after the manuscript's twentieth rejection. When Alice James Books accepted the collection on the condition that I replace the dull title, *My House in the Suburbs*, I was elated. That title had been my declaration of ordinariness, of lacking superpowers and nonsense names, and it's the title of a poem that struggles with the word "authentic," but I could see how its plainness might not sell books.

It took months to come up with "Middle Kingdom," which even after publication I feared was under- and overstated. It depends on the absence of *The* to suggest suburbia and Asian America as middles. It screams China. But it does describe the book's contents: American poems navigating the China-imagining that undergirds daily life for people perceived as East Asian in America, regardless of who they are, even at picture-book age. Some of the poems imagine a faraway land, as I did when reading *The Five Chinese Brothers*, without critical commentary; others show collisions between notions of Chinese America; others show notions of Chineseness and Americanness blurring in a person; still others don't mention race or nation at all but simply live their lives, like a child walking into a library, having no idea what adventures await, wanting only to embark.

2021

References

Bishop, Claire Huchet, and Kurt Wiese. *The Five Chinese Brothers*. New York: Coward-McCann, 1938.

Lin, Grace. *Rethinking Tikki Tikki Tembo*. April 6, 2012 blog post accessed April 18, 2021. http://www.gracelinblog.com/2012/04/rethinking-tikki-tikki-tembo.html

Moffett, Angela Christine. "Exploring Racial Diversity in Caldecott Medal-Winning and Honor Books" (2016). *Master's Theses*. 4699.
DOI: https://doi.org/10.31979/etd.8khk-78uy
https://scholarworks.sjsu.edu/etd_theses/4699

Mosel, Arlene, and Blair Lent, Jr. *Tikki Tikki Tembo*. New York: Macmillan, 1968.

Between the Shopping Cart and
the Chinese Restaurant

EVEN BEFORE the pandemic, I cooked most of the meals served in my house. Long-term membership in a CSA (community-supported agriculture) has forced me to keep pace with a steady stream of fresh produce and trained me to cook according to the season. Here in central Pennsylvania, where I live and teach in a small town two hours' drive from a major airport, I'm lucky to be surrounded by small producers of meat, eggs, produce, and grain, and to know how their workers, animals, and land are treated. Although I'm not all virtue in this department—I'm not vegan or vegetarian, and I'm not about to renounce coffee, chocolate, olive oil, Alaskan salmon, or spices from all over the world—I believe that favoring local, sustainably grown food is an ethical no-brainer. And yet I've been thinking, teaching, and writing about food for decades, and one reason the topic never feels finished is that the ethics of eating are too complex for any one principle to rule. Food choices are much more than a set of agricultural and ecological principles; eating is a living amalgam of hunger, desire, tradition, and rituals connected to the past and future.

There's one situation in which all sourcing questions go out the window for me: when I'm with extended family in an Atlanta Chinese restaurant: the large, bustling kind whose round tables serve as central gathering spots for families like mine. In such places, in communion with my relatives, I eat with abandon, suppressing all thoughts of polluted fish farms, overuse of herbicides and pesticides, and the CAFOs (concentrated animal feeding operations, notorious for inhumane conditions for both workers and animals, as well as devastating environmental effects) where the pork and beef were probably raised. Such restaurants, which can turn out a succession of dishes still exhaling the breath of the wok while a family converses uninterrupted, are a completely different world from one's home, where Chinese meals for more than a few people must either exclude the cook or be eaten after the wok has stopped breathing—and, too, a number of beloved dishes are impractical to make.

To me, an urban Chinese restaurant packed with families is a space outside time. Its raw materials have been transformed by a magical process that defies the question of where those materials came from. As a shopper in an Asian (or non-Asian) grocery store, I have misgivings about farmed shrimp, minimally labeled trays of meat, and all manner of packages lacking ingredient lists or expiration dates, but I will consume the same items without misgivings if they're presented—transformed by unseen professionals and still sizzling on the serving dish—on an outsized lazy Susan, around which my relatives are talking, laughing, and taking photos, each of us occupying just enough table space for a small rice bowl, saucer-size plate, and tiny teacup into which an infinite supply of oolong, Pu-Er, or chrysanthemum tea is poured. With my China-born cousins, the conversation jumps from English to Chinese to Chinglish, and every dish is shared. It is all togetherness, tradition, absorption, pleasure. On my trips to Atlanta, it's one of the events I look forward to most. Am I just weak? Or are there also ethical reasons to put aside what, in my own kitchen, I consider my values around food, such as holding out as often as possible for sustainable agriculture and humane treatment of livestock?

These restaurant meals have a ceremonial aspect that places them outside the normal stream of daily eating. Unless someone wants a drink other than hot tea, there is no individual ordering, so there is no deliberation over, or personal accountability for, an individual choice of entrée. If one person or household is hosting the meal—having invited the others to the restaurant and declared the non-negotiable intention to pay for it—the host composes the procession of dishes. And while it's acceptable to quietly skip a dish once things get busy, it's generally expected that everyone will partake of everything on the table, for the meal is a common experience jointly choreographed by host and chef.

The ritual goes like this: there may be small plates to start, such as smoked fish or fried peanuts, but there might not be. Soup can be first or last or both, brought out in a large bowl. The server arranges a line of individual bowls along the edge of the lazy Susan, ladles hot soup into each bowl, and lets each diner claim a bowl. Any remaining soup in the serving bowl stays, and it's good etiquette to press it on others until the chorus of refusals is settled by one or two people who, after a demurral or two, relent. Noodles and steamed fish tend to arrive late in the procession. In the middle can be almost anything: stir-fries of meat and vegetables, bubbling sandpot casseroles featuring tofu or shellfish or both, crisp salt-and-pepper squid adorned with hot chilies, a bright green heap of spinach flash-cooked with smashed garlic. When the lazy Susan gets crowded, someone must be persuaded to take the last prawn so that that serving dish can be removed; the middle-aged press the prawn on their elders, and the elders press it on their grandchildren. Since Chinese meals expand to include more people by increasing the variety of dishes (rather than the size of each dish), large gatherings see an acceleration. The first dish often arrives by itself, the next two together, and then, in a rush of movement, often with multiple servers, three or four show up simultaneously, creating happy chaos in the center of the table and rewarding all who have had the restraint not to overload on the first few.

Dessert is minimal: iconic orange slices are all but required, and on occasion, the kitchen sends a sweet soup: red (adzuki) bean or taro, possibly adorned with tapioca pearls. Red bean soup is dead simple to make—it can consist of as little as beans, water, and sugar—but I almost never make it, so its appearance at the table shakes something awake in me. Why don't I make it at home? Because I live where almost no one else makes it and few would accept it if offered? Because home and restaurant are separate spaces, in which different foods are expected? I am never too full for one of these soups, even when it comes as a surprise. Served in small quantities and not laden with butter or cream, they are easier to eat after a large meal than cake or pastry, and tea is already on the table.

In my non-churchgoing family, these gatherings may be the closest thing we have to a religious ritual. We have held these meals throughout my life, even before Chinese restaurants in Atlanta began tailoring their menus to Chinese customers by offering braised chicken feet and fish-maw soup, and before my parents, who each immigrated alone as a foreign student to Atlanta in the middle of the twentieth century, had extended family in the area. In the early days, we captured joy with Chinese American friends, early restaurant offerings (Moo Goo Gai Pan, Egg Drop Soup), and the then-ubiquitous zodiac placemats; fortune cookies were as close as we got to red bean soup. Later, my maternal grandparents, who had settled in Taiwan after fleeing the Communist takeover of Shanghai in 1949, came to the U.S. to retire in Atlanta. Around that same time, several cousins from mainland China arrived to the same area as graduate students. These were not isolated journeys: the city's Asian population was growing, so the Chinese restaurants multiplied, and the meals we enjoyed in them not only became larger gatherings but also offered dishes closer to what my cousins and grandparents had left behind. Even after I moved North for school and work, I went back to Atlanta regularly, my children and my cousins' children eventually replacing my late grandparents at the table. Restaurants and their rituals connected these children to the great-grandparents they never met, just as, during my early childhood, restaurants connected me to entire family networks I couldn't meet, due to frozen diplomatic relations between the U.S. and China.

My daughters and I rarely have such a meal in South-Central Pennsylvania, where I teach creative writing and where they were born. We have no family nearby, and the Chinese restaurant landscape is a lot like that of 1970s Atlanta: Chinese American standbys such as Sweet and Sour Pork, General Tso's Chicken, and combination plates with an egg roll and fried rice. One distinctly twenty-first-century aspect of our American restaurant world, however, is the "farm-to-table" establishment: the kind of place that lists local suppliers on the menu and adjusts its offerings with the seasons. Although I associate places like this with posh areas of major cities, they have also succeeded in smaller towns. My town, Carlisle, boasts 1794 The Whiskey Rebellion, where a burger made with bison from Gunpowder Farms costs $17.94; the "rod and reel caught Chesapeake Bay striped bass," $26.94. At The Millworks in nearby Harrisburg, a vegetarian entrée featuring local mushrooms and grits from Bucks County, Pennsylvania's Castle Valley Mill is $24.00; a serving of meatloaf made with local, grass-fed beef and paired with seasonal vegetables costs $25.00. These prices are more than fair. Wherever they are, farm-to-table restaurants—using costly, fragile, and inconsistently available ingredients—have little choice but to charge more than their conventional counterparts. Their reasons for such sourcing are usually ethical: sustaining land, supporting small farms, promoting humane treatment of animals, reducing the carbon footprint of a meal. The raw material has a high cost in dollars, and that cost is necessarily reflected on the tab.

I myself am neither rich nor poor, a liberal-arts-college professor and single parent, wealthier in education and job security than in dollars. I can buy an expensive chicken and cook it myself, but I can't often buy an expensive chicken that someone else has cooked and served, and eat it from plates someone else will wash, dry, and put away. To hold a restaurant's larder to the same standard as my own grocery-shopping ethic doesn't hold up, practically or morally. The pandemic revealed that restaurant-going of all kinds can be a social good, keeping people employed, enlivening neighborhoods, and sustaining sources of prepared food for those who can't cook for themselves. Filtering my restaurant list by my grocery-shopping standard would leave almost exclusively high-priced ones. If compelled, I could live that way by dining out no more than once a month: goodbye, takeout sushi; goodbye, spontaneous lunches with colleagues. But even if that were practical, if consuming is a form of voting, it strikes me as wrong to support only elite restaurants. Many more in the community are served and employed by affordable restaurants than by luxury ones. And would anyone, even if wealthy, want every meal out to be fine dining?

It's almost unnecessary to state that few Chinese restaurants in the U.S. would land in the fine-dining category. Chinese cuisine at its most vaunted can hold its own against French or Italian, possibly superseding both with its geographic diversity, but the American association between Chinese food and cheap takeout makes it difficult for high-end Chinese restaurants to survive; the very phrase "high-end Chinese restaurant" sounds alien to most American ears. This judgment, often unconscious, clings to the food of countries associated with low-paid immigrant labor. Scholar Krishnendu Ray has explored this phenomenon:

American taste-makers... have framed their appropriation of twentieth-century culinary cultures in two diver-
gent ways: first, as high-status foreign foods, initially
limited to Continental and French cuisines, eventually
consecrating Italian and Japanese cookery at the end
of the century. Second, as the low-status product of the
labor and implicit knowledge of the immigrant poor clas-
sified as ethnic fare. The appropriation of the first sort
is understood primarily in aesthetic terms of taste and
notions of skill, while the latter is understood as a matter of necessity, primarily in terms of undifferentiated
toil (Ray, *The Ethnic Restaurateur*, New York: Bloomsbury,
2016: 63).

Although there are individual exceptions, on average, few are willing to pay as much for a Mexican or Vietnamese restaurant meal as
for a French or Japanese one, even when the ingredients and labor
are equal.

The Chinese restaurants I love—the ones I grew up with and the
ones my children have grown up with, in holiday and non-holiday
gatherings with grandparents and cousins—are mostly run by
hardworking immigrants who operate on the thinnest of margins.
They can't afford to court only wealthy and special-occasion customers; they need everyone, in an everyday way. Their competitive
prices made dining out possible for my own family, even in the early
years. And so, if I announced to my family that I was opting out of
our New Year's dinner because the restaurant's pork isn't pastured,
I would indeed be taking a small stand on behalf of animal welfare
and the environment, but I'd also be chipping away at someone
else's American dream. And I would sound insufferable, unwilling
to eat the food of ordinary people, my own relatives included. I'd
also be rejecting the food my immigrant parents provided to me in
childhood.

Thus the muddying of my home-shopping ethic. The ingredients I buy now are different from the ingredients my mother bought while raising young children, for two simple reasons: the Chez Panisse-inspired passion for local, sustainably produced ingredients hadn't reached Georgia in the 1970s, so the choice wasn't there—and even if it had been, my family wouldn't have been able to afford the highest tier of groceries. That I can afford them now is a result of many circumstances. My parents' dedication to my education (and their parents' dedication to theirs) is one reason I'm in the professional class and doing what I love. Their frugal kitchen habits taught me to make the most of every ingredient, and sustainably grown foods, while more expensive than conventional, are more affordable and available than ever. So is cooking instruction, which can be found at little to no cost online, whereas, when I was a teenager interested in cooking, my mother took me to a used bookstore, where our scrounging yielded the unsuitable *Weight Watchers International Cookbook*. No one in the family was trying to lose weight, and the fundamental cooking instruction I wanted was not in it; I wasted time and ingredients trying to glean from its pages tips and training that the book was not designed to teach. In retrospect, I think my mother didn't want me to waste my talents in the kitchen, where most women of her generation had been stranded against their will. Her ambivalent response to my interest in cooking parallels the discouragement many of today's prominent Asian American chefs, raised in restaurant families, faced from their own parents, who in most cases had labored to spare their children the hardships of the industry: brutally long hours for little pay, almost no days off, general invisibility, the power dynamics of tipping. Working with food, as well as writing about it, has a respectability today that it lacked then.

One could argue that the restaurant industry is so full of hardships—ranging from worker exploitation to animal cruelty—that the ethical choice is to cook at home, but at some point, staying away from restaurants goes from conscientious consumption to creating one's own elite private dining room. As a result, it can be hard to know what to do in the supermarket. Before grocery stores shifted the work of scanning and bagging to their customers by offering handheld scanners and "self checkout," I used to stand in line behind my fellow shoppers and, whether I meant to or not, contemplated what they were buying and what that might reveal about their lives. Some carts were piled with mostly canned and boxed foods from the center of the store, while others were heaped with the more irregularly shaped packages of fresh produce, meat, and seafood from the periphery. Some shoppers had an abundance of store-brand items and a wad of coupons; others had organic, name-brand everything and extras like fresh flowers. My own shopping fell (and still falls) between the extremes, but at a glance, my cart leans elite, especially if one could see the CSA produce, meat, and milk that's not in my cart but is at home in the refrigerator—items that took extra time, another scarce resource, to gather separately.

On a practical level, I consider shopping like this the best I can do for the health of my family and the planet. But on the murkier level of trying to behave ethically: when the grass-fed, organic version costs twice as much as conventional and may require a separate errand, such shopping choices reek of snobbery. Although those choices could be seen as votes for sustainable agriculture, increasingly I'm part of a two-tiered system, in which those who can afford it buy one kind of food and those who cannot buy another. (There's potentially a third category, those who can afford the more expensive items but don't believe in them, but I put these people in the first category because they have a choice.) There was a spell in my adult life when I couldn't afford the upper tier, and I remember how it felt to look into the carts of those who could—an amorphous, simmering resentment—even though I had an Ivy League diploma and a few publications and knew my tight budget was likely to loosen one day. For those not anticipating a change in circumstances, that resentment surely does more than simmer, especially as the years go by without improvement in either income or healthful choices.

Between the shopping cart and the Chinese restaurant, I see my own childhood, during which everyone I knew drank regular (not organic or grass-fed) milk, crunched conventionally grown apples coated in wax to make them shine, and bought mass-produced chicken in foam trays at the supermarket. It was all we had; ground beef and canned tomatoes were the same for everyone. It was not a time of complete innocence—we now know the cost of how these products reached the shelves—but it was a time of abundance, especially for those who had fled home countries in which their families had lost everything. Even though I'm now accustomed to buying apples from the farmer who grew them, it's difficult to look back and consider one of the basic foods of my childhood contaminated. My parents built new lives in this country, in part because food was miraculously affordable and always available. At best, looking down on supermarket chicken and iceberg lettuce seems ungrateful.

So when I gather with relatives around a restaurant meal that at once evokes a distant land and builds new memories in the land we live in, I feel as if we're inhabiting a space outside time, a room that has always welcomed all of us, including the foreign-born in their first days in the U.S. The simple pleasure of eating together reminds me that the problems of the food industry are not mine alone to solve. I choose what seems right under each circumstance, and there are times when it makes more sense to be guided by feeling than by thought. At these gatherings, where we are in close proximity to other Asian American families having their own gatherings, I submit to the sense of celebration and eat what's put before me. Soon I'm lost in the ritual and the flavors that bring joy and affirmation: this family, scattered by revolutions, trans-Pacific migrations, and lengthy periods of separation, is thankful to be together, as they break bread more likely to be steamed than baked. How all the components of the meal got here is as complicated as how each of us got here. Humanly and imperfectly, bite by bite, we do the best we can.

2021

North and South

WHEN I LEFT my native Atlanta in 1985 for college up North, I was raring to get out of town. I wanted to be a poet, and the literary world was in New York and Boston.

Meeting people on campus often evoked surprise. "You're from Atlanta?" Classmates perceived Atlanta as *Gone with the Wind* or *Hee Haw*.

I explained: Atlanta was populated by people from everywhere. My lack of a Southern accent reflected it: in but not entirely of the South. I'd often been the only Asian person in the room, but Atlanta had an Asian population that was scattered, thus unseen.

Yet I *was* of the South. I called myself "Oriental." I smiled upon encountering another Asian person in public. I smiled in general. I didn't find Asianness and Southern accents incompatible, as I knew Chinese Americans whose families had inhabited small-town Georgia and Alabama for generations, as well as first-generation Americans like my parents, who came to Georgia as students in the 1940s and '50s.

Still, the urban intellectual North won me over. Offered only European languages before, I abandoned Latin and French for Chinese and Japanese. I replaced "The Far East" with "East Asia." At a dinner table spontaneously shared by Asian Americans, I laughed until I cried when a guy mimicked his grandfather's Japanese accent. I'd never heard such mockery delivered with love, to a group that could relate with appreciation.

Throughout my twenties—in New York, college towns, and art outposts—I felt delivered from my isolation as an aspiring poet in a business hub, as a Chinese American in a culture that deemed a person Chinese *or* American. Eventually, I landed an academic job in no city at all, but a small town two hours from a major airport.

I've lived in that town, Carlisle, Pennsylvania, population 19,000, ever since. I cherish my colleagues, students, and neighbors. I've raised two kids and written four books here. While I can't claim I haven't missed urban life, nor that every neighbor was welcoming, I still believe that wherever you go, most people are good.

Over the years I've watched with sadness as colleagues of color left for more diverse settings, even before the Trump years, which brought me an increase in racial harassment and hostile interactions without provocation. I've generally felt that my early experiences prepared me to live as a tiny minority. But last week, when three Asian-owned spas in and near Atlanta were attacked by a white gunman, killing eight people, six of them Asian women, everything flew into doubt. I've experienced numbness and pain, rage and despair, disbelief and awareness that I had expected this.

My job is safer than the jobs of spa employees, but I see anew how I coped with the pandemic under an openly racist president. When gyms closed and many took to walking for exercise, I cut back on going outside. After dark, I drove, even to travel two blocks. I appreciated the obscuring effect of masks.

As the wait for vaccination in Pennsylvania grew longer, the need to return to in-person classes more pressing, a friend sent a tip: one reason for the delay was a shortage of workers, and we could help. There was demand for educators and people to manage vaccination sites—and volunteers would be vaccinated. White friends signed up and got their shots. I wavered for weeks, worried that appearing at a COVID-related event would make me a target of violence. On March 16, I decided that any hate was likely to be verbal. It would be worse to get sick than be called something I'd surely been called before. Sticks and stones... I registered to volunteer. Six hours later, the first of the three shootings began.

I now realize that my small-town life has always had an urban dimension: trips to see family and inhabit vibrant Asian American spaces—in Atlanta. My home county of DeKalb, which counted 507 Asian residents in 1970, or about 0.1%, is now 6.5% Asian. Some areas are one-quarter Asian. My daughters and I love the international markets and food courts where Asians blend in, rather than stand out. In middle age, I finally feel like an ordinary person in the city of my birth.

And I should have known there would be a cost. As the pandemic raged and many in power blamed China for everything, attacks on Asians followed, often where there should be safety in numbers: New York, San Francisco. Atlanta's attainment of substantial racial diversity, which I found so exciting—my hometown, shedding its Scarlett O'Hara vibe!—had also made it a place where Asians, finally visible, were easily targeted.

I had just spent five years writing poems about Atlanta, so when lockdown began, I was primed to substitute mental for actual travel. Thus I hadn't connected the dots. I was dwelling in a vision of Atlanta reborn, a city where the two Asian kids in fourth grade don't avoid each other for fear of ostracism, where a lunch of Sichuan noodles is not alien but aspirational. The city where I was raised, in a loving home, in an area where most neighbors were welcoming. As long as my native soil retained that benevolent aura, if someone yelled "Go home!" from a truck window in Pennsylvania, the joke was on him because Atlanta was where I was headed, as soon as travel was safe.

2021

Invisible Cooks

Whoever packed the lunches at the conference or colony.
The boiler of tapioca pearls for the bubble tea.
The fryer of turnip cakes for the dim-sum cart.
Peelers of the garlic cloves that fill the jar.
Makers of the brownies at the piano recital.
Layerers of baklava for the Greek Festival.
Canners of jam in gingham at country markets.
Crafters of hand-pulled noodles, unless the place makes
    a show of it.
School cafeteria workers, the ones in the back.
Preparers of banchan, ahead of the bibimbap.
Packers of coolers for the soccer tournament.
Whoever wrapped the dates in bacon.
The juicers of oranges before the brunch.
The mincers of onions, with bandaged thumbs.

2023

THE DIVORCED KITCHEN

THE KITCHEN itself has never married, never divorced. But the kitchen, after divorce, becomes a different room. It has lost its charge. It asks you, at times, to do nothing. Its un-emptied dishwasher and unswept floor have no emotional force because no one is pretending they don't exist. It is a room in which you are sometimes alone, or alone with a book. In it, you sometimes hang out with an old friend until late at night, as if you both were twenty-something again, your marriages in the future rather than in the past.

The married kitchen had overflowed with activity: lunch-packing, lunch-unpacking, dinner prep during breakfast, breakfast cleanup during dinner prep. Sometimes it was joyful chaos, such as during a child's birthday party, all the other parents pitching in with food preparation and child supervision. Other times, such as in daily life, there was no community. The kitchen was a lonely outpost that couldn't keep up with its requirements, an airport with insufficient gates, forcing planes to waste time and fuel as they circled (and babies wailed). Tiny, cordoned off from the rest of the house, with a shallow sink and limited counter space, it was always backlogged in crucial areas: dirty dishes crowding the sink and countertops, dubious food in the fridge, overflowing trash. The kitchen itself had become a hungry, dirty child, pleading for attention it wasn't getting, day and night, and developing ailments because of that neglect. Under time pressure, you took care of your actual children before attending to the metaphorical one, but to do so, you needed the kitchen dozens of times a day, and it was seldom ready to serve.

Your mother's kitchen wasn't like this, but maintaining it cost your mother, who was more interested in art and literature than in recipes, many hours of each day.

Sylvia Plath, one of the earliest poets to light a fire in you, suggested in an early poem, "The Disquieting Muses," that her mother, "whose witches always, always / Got baked into gingerbread" had wasted her life. The speaker of the poem, the defiant daughter, is by contrast an artist. Poetry is sacred, cooking profane.

When you were a child, some mothers in the neighborhood felt that way about their own lives: they had gone to college, where they felt the spark of career ambitions, but after graduation they had married and settled into full-time domesticity, rendering their kitchens clean while limiting their professional options.

Your generation was supposed to be different. In college, you were excited to meet other aspiring writers. Occasionally a male classmate said, "I want to be a house-husband, so I'll be free to write all day." No female classmate uttered the equivalent. Your vision of becoming a writer involved an urban studio apartment crammed with books; even though you hoped for more than that, you couldn't picture anything beyond monkish solitude and the accumulation of manuscript pages.

Before you were married, in graduate school and the lean years surrounding it, the kitchen had been a place of leisure. Yes, you needed to eat, but you cooked also because it was interesting, rewarding, even fun. Friends often dropped in around dinnertime. You bonded with people who appreciated restaurant-rich cities, especially when you found these people in small towns, where they, like you, were trying to reproduce dishes they couldn't get in the provinces. You were a novice cook, but your friends were hungry and happy to eat whatever you had attempted to make.

Because you were following literary opportunities wherever they could be found, those were also years of frequent moving. Every kitchen was rented. You and your peripatetic friends discussed the problem of acquiring books: the urge to build a personal library versus the need to fit everything into a U-Haul, again and again. Consensus: Poetry books and cookbooks were most worth owning. Unlike novels, they were never finished and could yield a different experience with each encounter.

In retrospect, the era of learning to cook resembles something from a bygone era: preparation for the day you would be a married woman turning out meals for a husband and children. At the time, you didn't see your cooking that way because the idea was retrograde, your menus worldly. When you eventually got engaged and set up a registry at Williams-Sonoma, your lack of originality became obvious. Cooking, whatever it had been, had also been practice for the day the stakes were higher, the day you were feeding a family and not a pack of aspiring artists who would be fine without your lamb and white bean stew, your seafood lo mein—people who gathered, often late into the night, to talk about books and paintings and other artists, and not just to be fed.

After you married and had children, your love for them turned out to be bigger than any kitchen you ever viewed on Houzz; your desire to cook for them, and to teach them to cook, drove you to spend many hours in your not-so-great kitchen, enjoying their learning and pleasure even as you inevitably dropped a shrimp or Brussels sprout into the half-inch gap between the stove and lower cabinet, or took a casserole out of the oven and could find nowhere to set it down. As the kids gained stature and skills, you remembered them as babies, unable to eat solid food, and how miraculous it seemed that one day you would sustain them with vegetables, grains, and the flesh of fish and birds and pigs, and not just with your own body, which at times made too much milk, making leaving the house a challenge, and at other times was too taxed to produce any food at all.

After some time as a divorced mother, you start dreaming up plans for a new kitchen, the limitations on space and budget functioning like the generative constraints of a received poetic form. This kitchen will understand your cooking style, the needs of a one-parent family, the power of organization. You have over a hundred spice jars, and now you'll be able to find the one that's called for. You will never again have to rummage for the roasting pan because it will soon have a designated home, as will other large objects such as the pizza peel and half-sheet pans.

The house is over a century old, so during renovation, horse-hair plaster dust wafts everywhere, even into sealed-off rooms and the insides of cabinets. It sneaks between stacked plates, into the cavities of upside-down wine glasses. Coming home from work, you have to wash every dish before using it, wipe down each chair before sitting in it. Since you typed all day, your wrists throb from overuse, but you've been through worse pain than this, and—as the childbirth instructors said—pain with a purpose is more bearable than pain alone.

Whether you're making light changes like repainting or doing major surgery such as moving plumbing and electricity, a kitchen needs no anesthesia. Yet it often seems like a human entity. It has psychic resonance. At night, it evokes your childhood home. In that kitchen, when you couldn't sleep, your mother stayed up with you and prepared a snack: a cut apple, a bowl of chicken noodle soup, a steamed bun filled with tiny chunks of glazed roast pork. In pre-microwave days, and sometimes even in the microwave era, your mother heated the bun on the stove, on a collapsible steamer basket nestled in a Revere Ware pot.

Today that pot is with you, consigned to the craft room, because in your era, All-Clad had displaced Revere Ware as the cookware of wedding registries, and you couldn't be bothered to polish the Revere Ware's copper bottom. When you spot the old pot among paintbrushes and glue, you silently thank your mother for staying up with you when she surely could have used some sleep.

The kitchen feels like a living thing, responsive to input, functional, sometimes even intelligent, but it lacks memory. It has no idea that there were kitchens before it—rented ones in university towns and in cities—or that long ago, in one of the rental kitchens, you accidentally cooked the meal your aunt had promised the recipe for. "When you find the man you want to marry," she had said, "call me and I'll give you the recipe that will make him propose."

The remodel is a commitment to being present for your children, for the friends you'll invite over for dinner, and for cooking itself, which at times is a passion, other times a burden. The people you feed are always grateful. Hosting a gathering, you can now go back to the kitchen for another bottle of wine or a serving utensil without pausing the conversation, because that dividing wall—which also made it difficult to keep an eye on young children while washing dishes or cutting up a chicken—is gone. Friends have seen you through hard times; having them over is a balm. It's worth all the money, all the days without a kitchen sink, all the fine dust.

Somehow, during the years of marriage, you got good at making Thanksgiving dinner. Most of those feasts were cooked with a baby or toddler or both nearby, your teaching duties in full swing. You started days in advance, baking the cornbread for the stuffing, chilling the dough for pie crust, chopping and toasting the pecans, picking up the turkey directly from the farmer. Thanksgiving may be a large meal, but most of its components can sit, pre-assembled, awaiting the oven. They are the opposite of most Chinese dishes, which cook briefly over a high flame and demand to be served the minute the wok exits the stove.

You used to cook Thanksgiving dinner for your parents or in-laws, all of whom lived far away; some years, when they didn't visit, you made the meal for local friends. Everyone brought wine, flowers, food; countertops and ovens were never so laden. The chaos was delicious, even though the kitchen was cramped and seques-tered, even though you sometimes barely got to eat. You kissed the top of your toddler's head and felt sustained by family and commu-nity. You remembered being twenty-two, alone in New York City, learning to cook from books, learning (the hard way) the lifespan of the chards and lettuces you had bought at the Union Square Greenmarket. It was a marvel that that young adult who had left home with few skills in kitchen management was now a mother, roasting large birds without anxiety, rolling out pie dough, creating warm fall memories for her children while advancing on the tenure track. You thought the holiday would go on like this indefinitely.

When you start dating again, you realize that fluency in cooking does not make it a gift to be given lightly. You've cooked for peo-ple in so many contexts—dinner parties, home-cooked meals delivered to new parents, children's friends staying over—that you nearly forgot what it means to cook for a love interest. You're picky about ingredients, carefully choosing tender early lettuces, oranges at their wintry peak, local eggs with firm, bright-orange yolks. Cooking communicates willingness to take care of another adult, to provide in an essential, everyday way, to set your own interests aside on an ordinary day, then another ordinary day, and then another, because it is worth it, because being together nourishes you both.

In Heather Clark's *Red Comet: The Short Life and Blazing Art of Sylvia Plath*, which relates the life of the iconic poet in minute detail, the young Sylvia seems always to be going out for dinner with another suitor. In a restaurant with one, she orders steak. In another restaurant with another, she orders steak again. Sylvia's mother, widowed when her daughters was eight, had raised her children alone since then. Steak was nutritious and often out of reach. A young woman who wanted to be a published poet and a mother was striving for a life she could find no living examples of. Why shouldn't she order what she wanted, something she couldn't always have, when it was offered?

Red Comet makes you stop focusing on Sylvia's despair in the final months, on the entwining of her death with her kitchen. Instead, you imagine her life, in restaurants, in libraries, in her country home when her marriage was happy. You see her at her typewriter and at her mailbox, where checks for her poems streamed in as her career took off, and you're better able to sit alone at your own kitchen table, scribbling in a notebook, revising, revising some more, and sending out.

The divorced kitchen has a peculiar collection of dishes. Its place settings—of which you have half a set—are too high-end to replenish on your own. They are also too beautiful and functional to lose. You buy a practical, average set from a nondescript department store, and now your table is a mishmash—not that you often need twelve place settings, but with six, you used to run out of dishes before the dishwasher was full.

Nobody who has come over has ever cared about coordinated place settings. In the early years, you and your friends cooked together because no one could afford to go out. A ragtag collection of plates, bowls, forks, knives, and chopsticks—gleaned from thrift shops and family downsizing—enhanced the group's sense of being nonconformist, resourceful, destined for artistic uniqueness.

Now, with all the trappings of adulthood, your friends still don't care what the plates and cutlery look like. Your generation rejects the family silver, the family china, and pristine dining and living rooms; eBay is bursting with vintage formal place settings. What matters is the everyday, which life is made of—a principle you knew intellectually but now know viscerally, and it's the everyday—in all senses of the word—that demands attention.

You have two talents, writing and cooking. Writing, when it succeeds and is published, eventually reaches people, most of whom you will never meet. Cooking reaches people in your vicinity, immediately. Not reaching readers would disappoint you. Not reaching actual people at your table would make you miserable. Your intention to live fully was written out in the floor plan for the kitchen, then made real. That room, the heart of the house, now meets your specifications. It's more than a symbol of your life; it *is* your life. You have no excuse not to inhabit it.

2023

ON LIKING TO COOK

Do you like to cook?

At home?
I like to cook when I'm not hungry yet. When the sink and dishwasher are clear. When I've had time to write and think earlier in the day and there's room in my head to listen to something low-stakes, whether music or a podcast, as I chop onions or grate ginger. When I'm making something familiar but not so familiar that making it becomes rote repetition. When I'm trying out something new, with leisurely curiosity and clear instructions. When good friends are coming over, the kind of friends who aren't bothered by mail and backpacks by the door, by mismatched forks, by writing notebooks on which I've spilled cooking oil and jam.

In an artists' colony?
I've always thought so, and I like cooking with others, but when looking for writing residencies, I apply only to those where every meal is prepared for the artists. Cooking is an outlet, and sometimes a creative one, but it's also a relentless requirement. The need to fit it around everything else, the cleanup it requires afterwards, the periodic fridge and freezer cleanouts drain away much of the joy I normally feel in creating a meal for people I care about, in transforming a pile of materials into something ready to enjoy. At

a colony, where strangers become good friends, where most hours are spent doing what regular life crowds out, when I walk into the dining room after a full day of writing and see dinner already made, my eyes sting with gratitude and joy and a touch of sadness—a sense of loss in the knowledge that regular life has never been, and will never be, even a little bit like this.

After breakfast or morning coffee, the artists reach into the communal fridge for snacks to take to their studios, where we spend our days in solitude, trying to capture something we're not sure we'll recognize, pushing past doubt, violating our original intentions, forgetting—if we ever knew—how to make small talk or fill out tax forms. Often, the best, most convenient snack for getting through those hours is a hard-boiled egg.

I like watching a poet or musician walk out of the kitchen holding an egg, often in bare hands, as if cradling a tiny ball of potential on the way to its crucible. Later, at dinner, the egg is gone, and a new song has come into the world.

In a bookstore?

I'm in the cookbook section not because I need another cookbook—I have hundreds—but because a life-changing volume may reside on these shelves. My life has been changed by books before. I used to feel guilty when I went straight to the cookbook section of a bookstore, skipping the poetry section because I wasn't in the mood for it, but no more. It's a false divide. Over the years, both cookbook-reading and cooking have sometimes—often—turned into poems.

There are also days when I make a beeline for the poetry section and don't pause to browse the cookbooks. My bookstore behavior changes like appetite. Sometimes you're in the mood for sweet food or savory, Asian food or Western, a casserole or a salad. Everything belongs to a larger whole. Everything nourishes the person and the art. The key is to listen to your inclinations and intuitions on a given day and treat them with respect, not suspicion. To have faith that the interests that tug at you, as long as they're constructive, will coalesce into something with meaning.

In the community?
I *think* I like to cook, which is why I have a hard time saying no when asked to cook for someone I don't know well who has had a baby or a family emergency. I'm generally regarded as a person for whom cooking is easy. I'll admit I have the experience and equipment. But I'm also a person who tends to forget the limits of her resources and promise too much. I have caught myself assembling casseroles at 1 a.m. while my children slept and a full day of teaching awaited, because I couldn't say no to the meal-train invitation, where the signup page showed that nearly every local woman I know, along with a couple of men, had volunteered.

Maybe because my parents never made me feel deprived while they were establishing themselves in this country, my default setting is to forget the areas in which I lack resources. Even when I lived alone with toddlers, I gave lemon tarts, chicken teriyaki, Chinese pork dumplings, lasagna, chicken noodle soup, miso-glazed salmon, yellow cake with chocolate ganache. I made the broth from chicken carcasses and vegetables, made the tart crust from butter, flour, sugar, salt, and egg yolks. I bought foil catering trays in bulk because I expected to deliver more, until a friend who'd seen me stressing out after volunteering one time too many ordered me to stop buying them.

Still, I love the moment of delivering the meal. I enjoy giving people food, whether they're guests in my house or I'm leaving dinner on the front porch while they adjust to a major life transition. Even for people I know only remotely, members of the same local community, I enjoy that gesture enough that I sometimes forget what that moment is going to cost—that at many points in life, cooking well is a leisure activity, and as things stand now, leisure is almost unheard of. That I need to change my life.

On Thanksgiving?
Not if the task is to repeat the exact Thanksgiving dinner I made last year and the year before. Thanksgiving channels tradition, but tradition doesn't have to mean ironclad duplication. I'm a teacher and creative writer; I'm all about learning, about discovering my own mind, about helping others discover theirs, about getting lost in the process of making something and being surprised. As soon as I find that, in writing, I'm engaged in repetition, as opposed to "theme and variation," I have to pull back and ask myself why I'm not doing better. Sometimes these questions result in silence, for a time.

In many social circles, people with a reputation for cooking well don't get invited to dinner because others find us intimidating to cook for. Please know that I'm not judging, that I don't regard cooking as competition. Please invite me, even if you're still learning to cook. I'll help if you want, or hold back. Even on Thanksgiving, I am delighted to be a guest, bringing wine and a side. Or wine and flowers.

In the first kitchen?
My mother, for whom it was never optional, did not like to cook, which gave me space. But she taught me to eat—to appreciate and be curious about new flavors and textures, and not to be repelled by pungent smells or unfamiliarity. She encouraged my love of bookstores and libraries, although the cooking section was not what she had in mind. She knew how to eat things the cookbooks didn't address—sour dried plums, tinned marinated eel, pork "fluff" sprinkled on congee—assertive, almost overpowering foods that demanded moderation and accompaniment.

She did not like to entertain because it stressed her out. The house always felt too messy, the good dishes too thoroughly packed and stored, the rituals of Chinese cooking tyrannical, with everything demanding to be served straight from the wok, one dish after another, still emanating steam. Although the canon includes stewed and cold dishes, it is by and large a cuisine in which cooking and eating take place simultaneously, so the cook cannot take part in conversation or even keep her clothes clean.

Often, the passion for cooking skips a generation. I think it's sometimes ignited in a young person by clear surfaces, the absence of meat marinating in the fridge and bread dough rising on the counter, the absence of other cooks in the kitchen, and the complete set of wine glasses—acquired through a wedding registry—dustless and pristine, waiting to be employed by friends, waiting to be decimated by mishaps among those friends, everyone scrambling for a paper towel or a wad of napkins, to soak up the spill, which for no known reason is always red.

Fundamentally, for people you love?
Yes.

2023

5

Interviews and a few poems

Substitutions

Balsamic, for Zhenjiang vinegar.
Letters, for the family gathered.

A Cuisinart, for many hands.
Petty burglars, for warring bands.

A baby's room, for tight quarters.
Passing cars, for neighbors.

Lawn-mower buzzing, for bicycle bells.
Cod fillets, for carp head-to-tail.

Children who overhear the language,
for children who speak the language.

Virginia ham, for Jinhua ham,
and nothing, for the noodle man,

calling as he bears his pole
down alley and street, its baskets full

of pickled mustard, scallions, spice,
minced pork, and a stove he lights

where the customer happens to be,
the balance of hot, sour, salty, sweet,

which decades later you still crave,
a formula he'll take to the grave.

Interview with Wendy Chin-Tanner for
The Lantern Review, 2012

WCT: In the 1990s, you participated in the slam poetry revival, even going to the nationals for the NYC team in 1991. How did you move from the poetry slam world to your current place in academia?

AS: I fell into the poetry slam by accident when I was too young to have a writerly identity and the slam was too young to have specific expectations of contestants. There was less of a page-stage divide. I saw no contradiction in reading my poems at the Nuyorican while sending them to university-based literary journals. The Nuyorican was a revelation. I'd never experienced writing in such a social way before. So while it may look as if I made a major transition over the years, I was really pursuing what I loved all along in whatever venues would have me. The people I met in both worlds had the same passions, though they may have been expressed differently on the surface.

Getting into academia was a different story: you don't get an academic job by accident. Even there, though, I thought my presence might be temporary. I started out as a sabbatical replacement and only gradually began to identify myself as a member of academia. Departing from the slam scene happened organically: I no longer lived in a city, I had children, and the slam itself had changed, requiring acting skills. Not long ago, I went back to the Nuyorican and saw a whole new generation of poets doing what "we" were doing twenty years earlier. It was terrific. For me, its time had come and gone.

WCT: You have stated in the past that your days in slam poetry taught you the value of connecting with people through the spoken word and reaching the non-university audience. How do you maintain that sense of the social in your work now?

AS: I think I do this mainly by continuing to write poems that on some levels can be read by anyone.

WCT: Poetry of the academy and poetry that is accessible to non-literary audiences are often perceived as contradictory. As a poet of the academy with a spoken-word past, how do you reconcile the two?

AS: I think I address this somewhat in question one, but I might add that academic institutions can also be great home bases for students to create spoken-word events. Dickinson students are doing this. I'd also suggest that as educators, we don't have to treat "page" and "spoken-word" poems the same way in class. Some poems you need to pick apart. Some you can just listen to or watch, and discuss in a different way: that too is instructive. The poems that don't need much interpretation can be the hardest to use in class. That requires some adaptation on the part of the teacher.

WCT: Parenting is a common subject in your poems. How do you balance being a working poet and a parent?

AS: Time management cubed. Electronic reminders. Lunch at my desk.

WCT: After publishing three books of poems, what strategies have you found for moving from one book to another? How do you know when one book is finished and when the next is ready to begin?

AS: I think I'm better at telling when one is finished than telling when a new one is ready to begin. The latter is much more difficult: you're casting about in the void unless there's a plan in place, which there rarely is. That said, I did have a plan for *Having None of It*.

WCT: Your last two books have been published by Manic D Press, while your first was published by Alice James Books. Though both Manic D and Alice James are small presses, each has a distinctly unique ethos. Can you talk about the experience of working with two different presses of different sizes and—presumably—of different editorial viewpoints? What attracted you to each of them? What advice would you give to young poets about selecting presses to which to send their work?

AS: I was drawn to both for their devotion to the work, to keeping their books in print. AJB's two-year work commitment was perfect for where I was at the time; even if I lived in the region now, I would have a much harder time traveling for regular meetings and reading manuscripts. Manic D has a freshness and irreverence that I love. It's all about the work—and perhaps it's in keeping with my poetry-slam past, which indeed is how Manic D and I made our first acquaintance (through their *Poetry Slam* anthology).

WCT: The poems in *Having None of It* weave in and out of the weighty topics of immigration and family history with a lightness of touch, as in "Imagining China" and "Inheritance." Similarly, you imbue lighter poems based on pop cultural experience, such as "Ode to a Lipstick," "Even the Overachievers Had Barbies," and "T.J. Maxx," with deeper and darker layers of meaning. These poems seem to insist on the multiplicity of identity, that each individual has a multitude of facets—mother, lover, daughter, Chinese, American, academic, consumer, subject, and object. I am fascinated by your exploration of "otherness"—both in terms of gender and in terms of culture. Can you talk a bit about how these critical and political concerns bleed over into more practical considerations of craft?

AS: Thank you for seeing the lightness and heaviness, which I do intend. Still, I may be the worst person to talk about these craft questions, as most of these things happened organically. When I was growing up, I didn't see it as ironic that while I was viewed as Chinese, I knew no Chinese and thrived on the study of Latin. Non-Western languages and literature were not there for me to study. In college, I indulged my interest in them, taking Chinese and Japanese but on some level longing to be in the English department. Everywhere I went, I was half in another place. It's perfect displacement for being a poet.

WCT: The poems in *Having None of It* possess an effortlessness and simplicity of language that belies a rigorous experimentation with form. Some poems adhere more firmly to form, as in the blank verse couplets of "Inheritance," and others deal with it more loosely, as a jazz musician might, as in the slant rhymes of "Having It All." How is your relationship with form evolving through your career?

AS: I worry that it isn't evolving, that I'm somehow wedded to it. I keep promising myself I'm going to depart from form, but I keep going back. It's how I find my way.

WCT: With the emergence of more Asian American poets in the field than ever before, audiences are becoming more accustomed to reflections of the Asian American experience. Do you perceive any changes in the way that identity is being dealt with in Asian American poetry, and in the way Asian American poets are being read? Has this affected the way you write and think about identity in your own writing?

AS: It's becoming more of a normal topic. This is good. It frees me and other Asian American poets to address it without necessarily making an issue of it. It lets identity be just one more dimension of a poem, rather than its reason for being.

WCT: Can you tell us about what you're working on now?

AS: My manuscript is—and I may be wrong here—about whether we shape our lives or they're fated. I know that sounds ridiculous. Writers have been addressing this since before the printed word. But that's what I'm preoccupied with. Some of the poems are about food, others on love, others on laundry. What life is made of.

2012

Interview with Rick Barot for
New England Review, 2017

RB: When you submitted your poems to us, you mentioned that they are part of a long project that centers on food. Can you say more about the project as a whole, and about the two poems in *NER* in particular?

AS: This collection-in-progress began with the realization that my hometown, Atlanta, is turning into what I wished it was in my youth: an international city where large immigrant communities thrive, many languages are spoken, and food—whether at home or in restaurants—reflects that worldliness. Buford Highway, which in my teenage years was just one more of the obscure places my family went for dim sum, is now a foodie destination noted for stretches of signs in Chinese, Vietnamese, Spanish. For the most part, I'm glad about that. Having lived in small-town Pennsylvania for 17 years, I count on eating Chinese food whenever I go to Atlanta to see family.

In Chinese American terms, what makes the city's transformation bittersweet is that it was built on the mostly-invisible efforts of the earliest immigrants, including my parents, who, at least racially, were pioneers. My father arrived in 1948, when the still-segregated city did not know what to do with people neither white nor Black.

My mother arrived in the mid-1950s, not yet having met my father. Each grew accustomed to being the only "Oriental" person in the room, or one of few. Although both came from families with connections to the West, they had to re-create themselves while eating biscuits and gravy, and they did so successfully.

They gave me a great life. Maybe this is true of all people with good parents: they made home feel permanent, safe, and abundant with good food. They also developed a network of Chinese American friends whose homes, though scattered in various white suburbs, were our homes, too. So I've never gotten over the injustice that their generation has grown old, many have passed away, and many of the kids have settled elsewhere, causing the houses to be sold. How could this be? Weren't we going to have spring-roll parties in these kitchens forever, and run into each other at the good Chinese restaurants? And what are all those hipsters doing in our restaurants?

Of course, all of this is normal, the passage of time, the American story, but it's no less difficult for being the standard course of history. I started writing these poems when I realized that food was the best metaphor for this experience. Food is at the center of Chinese gatherings; food was the only thing I already understood when, in college, I studied abroad in Taiwan and China; losing beloved foods is one of the most poignant aspects of migration; and mainstream American foods of the 1970s—the kind we demean now—were also a formative part of my life.

"Substitutions" [p. 193] was prompted by my reading of Fuchsia Dunlop's introduction to a recipe for Dan Dan Noodles in her Sichuan cookbook *Land of Plenty*—a beautiful evocation of street-vendor cooking. For me it merged with other memories of street vendors my parents have cited, as well as my experiences with street food as a foreign student in Shanghai, in an era surely now lost there, too.

"That Almond Dessert" [p.205] arose from my reading of Chinese American cookbooks from the 1960s. Somewhere I stumbled across the name "Almond Junket" and found it irresistible. That sent me to the *Joyce Chen Cook Book*, which my mother used when I was a child, and which evoked a longing for Almond Float—although I wasn't sure whether I actually longed for it or just wanted childhood back. Eventually I made a batch, then another and another. I still love it and consider it a partner for canned fruit, but I'd rather have it with canned lychees or longan than fruit cocktail.

RB: Reading your poems, I was reminded of works by other writers—Maxine Hong Kingston, Don DeLillo, Li-Young Lee, James Joyce, and Gertrude Stein immediately came to mind—where food is a crucial way of delving into themes like authenticity, nostalgia, desire, belonging, exile. As you wrote your food poems, what themes arose for you?

AS: I'm honored by your list of literary giants. Writing these poems has been immensely satisfying. I've had a long preoccupation with both food and poetry but never so wholeheartedly brought them together. All of the themes you mention arise constantly, especially authenticity and nostalgia, both of which are prone to illusion and romanticizing. Exile is a major one. Other themes: the importance of ritual (both the progression of courses in a Chinese meal and, say, the habit of relying on instant ramen to get through a day), ideas of community (all of us belong to many, and it's not always self-evident which ones), class (which overlaps with being an immigrant), power relationships (especially concerning cooking and domestic work), and always loss: in a way, this project is an elegy for a now-elderly generation of Chinese immigrants who embraced Atlanta, and embraced the South, early on, despite the region's reputation for racism—a reputation that drove most to favor New York and California.

RB: "Substitutions" and "That Almond Dessert" show your exqui-site skill with rhyme. Can you speak about rhyme's appeal for you? And who are the poets whose rhyming—or, more broadly, their musicality—you admire?

AS: Thank you! Rhyme helps me draft and rewrite a poem; with-out it, I easily lose my way or never find it to begin with. I also rely on a rhyme scheme to keep my mind from reaching a too-logical conclusion or leaning too heavily on voice. And having a formal scheme, even a loose one, helps me know when a poem is finished. Writing free verse is more difficult for me, as there are too many choices. Often, all look equally good.

A few beloved rhyming poets: Seamus Heaney, Donald Justice, Maxine Kumin, Randall Mann, Paul Muldoon, Molly Peacock. I went to the University of Virginia for graduate school because I heard Rita Dove read "Parsley" in 1988 or so; also at UVa, Charles Wright taught me a large proportion of what I know about form. Also, I spent a good chunk of high school clumsily trying to trans-late the *Aeneid*, which was a good, long lesson in meter.

RB: This last question has become a standard closing question for me, because I'm always eagerly making lists of new things to read and listen to and see. Who or what are you recommending to others these days?

AS: Carol Ann Duffy's *The Bees*, especially as they buzz around in my backyard these days (and I hope they will continue to, despite what looks like climate apocalypse on the way). My late friend Claire Kageyama-Ramakrishnan's last collection of poems, *Bear, Diamonds and Crane,* which I wish I could discuss with her, as it plumbs family history without sentimentality. My colleague Susan Perabo's wry and wrenching new novel, *The Fall of Lisa Bellow.* My recent colleague Elise Levine's new novel, *Blue Field,* written in language as compressed as poetry. James Baldwin's *Notes of a Native Son*, which I wish I had read decades ago. The soundtrack to "Hamilton."

Anne Mendelson's *Chow Chop Suey* is the most engaging history of Chinese American food I've found in my background work. That it was written by someone not fluent in Chinese is astounding, given its authority on food terminology in multiple Chinese dialects (each a language, Mendelson argues, in its own right). It puts in perspective a multitude of forces—among them the worldliness and resourcefulness of the earliest Cantonese immigrants to the U.S. during the Gold Rush, China's ancient tradition of restaurants, American discrimination through the Chinese Exclusion Act (in effect from 1882 to 1943), and racially motivated mob violence—that shaped the dishes most commonly found in American Chinese restaurants. *Chow Chop Suey* relates this history with the storytelling power of a novel; its postscript, "What Might Have Been," dares to imagine that same period of Chinese immigration to the U.S. without the political and economic persecution. It turns my current efforts at writing poems upside down in the best ways.

2017

That Almond Dessert

We must have known it as Almond Float, thanks to Joyce Chen.
Indeed, it floated in the fruit cocktail, the maraschino cherries
as treasured as the tender white cubes that have so many names,

I no longer know which we used, the nomenclature muddled
    further
by my later learning to say *xingren doufu,* which translates
to Almond Tofu, a reference not to what it is, but to how it
    appears.

For similar reasons, or to clarify for guests, we sometimes called it
Almond Jell-O, despite Jell-O's omission, to this day, of the flavor.
Meanwhile, restaurants may have offered it as Almond Junket

for its likeness to the English dessert made from milk and rennet,
junket having come from the Latin *iuncata,* reed basket, in which
cheese was made, and from which the Italian soft cheese *giuncata*

gets its name, all of which is not inaccurate because—contrary
to what they say about the Chinese and dairy—there was milk in
    ours, too.
This potentially put it closer to pudding than tofu, but its silky

texture evoked the most delicate bean curd, which may be why
it was also known as Almond Curd, which confusingly implies
that almonds can curdle, that somewhere lies an Almond Whey.

In any case, pudding lacks shape and makes a poor reference
for a Chinese audience. Perhaps to erase all cultural confusion,
the dessert also went by Almond Lake, as anyone can comprehend

a body of water in which something cool and almondy
is suspended. Looking back, Almond Junket is the only name
we never used, surely because it sounded like an illicitly

funded cruise or evoked the notion of a junk, which made us feel
foreign, pertaining to trash. But now fruit cocktail is what gets
consigned to the heap, canned foods being spurned unless you seal

and boil each jar yourself. And something about a sweet finale
aligned with gratuitous travel enchants, promising a destination
remote and novel, or remote and familiar, like ancient memory.

Interview with Aspen Matis for
The Best American Poetry blog, 2021

AM: What is poetry's greatest role in your inner life? Why do you write poems?

AS: Writing poems is the most difficult and original thing I'm capable of doing. It uses all of my intellectual resources, as well as whatever small abilities I might possess in music, visual art, storytelling, and the many languages I've studied but can't speak. Also, I find that writing a poem reduces the pain of nagging uncertainties, not by providing certainties, but by putting a question or problem into comprehensible form.

AM: What is the most radical thing a poet can do in his or her work?

AS: First, to make our everyday vocabulary do something no one previously thought it could. Usually this has something to do with the roots of words, the root of "radical" being *radix*, "root." Second, to keep at poetry regardless of the recognition that does or doesn't appear in the poet's lifetime.

AM: This past March, you wrote a powerful and wrenching opinion-editorial in *The Atlanta Journal-Constitution* about how "As the pandemic raged and many in power blamed China for everything, attacks on Asians followed." In the context of the horrific racially-motivated Atlanta mass-shooting of Asian women, your essay shares a glimpse of your own experience as an Asian American woman from Atlanta. Relaying the ways in which you've navigated the rise in hostility and discrimination you've experienced in the past months, you write: "My job is safer than the jobs of spa employees, but I see anew how I coped with the pandemic under an openly racist president. When gyms closed and many took to walking for exercise, I cut back on going outside. After dark, I drove, even to travel two blocks. I appreciated the obscuring effect of masks." What moved you to write this very personal op-ed, and what impact do you hope your words will have?

AS: Thank you for this response to the piece. I wrote it because the news of the shooting left me feeling pinned by a boulder, and my initial efforts to roll it away—donating money, attending a rally—gave no relief. The boulder didn't budge. Its weight was saying that I was not only capable of more, the task was also non-optional. Jennifer Joseph of Manic D Press, publisher of three of my books, gave me the needed nudge. As an Asian American writer who not only grew up in Atlanta but was one week from publishing a book of poems centering Asian American Atlanta, I would be wrong not to speak up—and I needed to do it in a genre that moves faster and is more widely read than poetry. How long would the media be interested in Asian America? One, two weeks? If enough writers took up the cause, that interest could last longer. Strong op-eds by other Asian American writers were appearing by the day, so I also knew I needed to say something others hadn't already said. In terms of speed, I'm the opposite of a journalist, so even with Jen and other writer friends responding to drafts, and with every obligation I could cancel canceled, that short piece took me four full days of obsessive writing and rewriting. My hope is that it conveys something others may have wanted to say about being Asian American in a time of pandemic and racial unrest but didn't have the writing experience, access to publishing, or possibly even the English language to express—and that that makes a constructive difference, on any scale.

AM: Your most recent book of poems, *Peach State*, explores Atlanta, Georgia's transformation from the mid-twentieth century to today, as seen and shaped by Chinese Americans. Poet and critic Mark Jarman describes the collection as "elegant, lucid, formally inventive," and poet Paisley Rekdal calls the book "sly, smart and accessible, formally sophisticated and moving," adding that *Peach State* is "a beautiful and thought-provoking meditation on food, race, and identity." What would you like to share about the origins, creation process, and ambitions of this newest collection?

AS: In 2015 I saw how international Atlanta had become; being of Asian descent there was no longer the lonely condition I remembered from the 1970s. Both of these things had become clear to me through food: restaurants, grocery stores. In the early days, my family had simply done without many Chinese ingredients, but every now and then someone arrived with a suitcase full of treasures from New York, San Francisco, Taiwan, or Singapore. Today I'm the one who brings a suitcase full of treasures home to central Pennsylvania—from Atlanta. I wanted to write about these changes because, while Atlanta's transformation was what I had wanted all along, it also meant the erasure of an era. I wanted to acknowledge and celebrate the Chinese Americans, including my parents, who were there many years before the Immigration and Nationality Act of 1965 inadvertently created major demographic shifts. I found that I was best able to portray their resourcefulness, creativity, loneliness, and joy through food. They laid a path for the substantial Asian population of today's Atlanta—which I also wanted to celebrate. The writing process was a mixture of mourning and delight.

AM: Do the best books win the poetry prizes? Why do great works so often fall through the cracks of our literary foundation, into obscurity?

AS: When I look at shortlists, even longlists, for prizes, I think there is no "best" book. The books are usually doing different things and aren't meant to be compared to each other. That's why I think it's so important that independent publishers and university presses stay around; they care most about the integrity of the work, and while they certainly need to sell books, they aren't in it for the immediate public response. One day the overlooked great works may receive the recognition they deserve because someone kept them in print. *The Best American Poetry* is a great vehicle for that, too, putting both known and unknown poets' names in public libraries everywhere.

AM: Do you have any wisdom or guidance you'd like to share with young poets?

AS: Have faith that your non-literary talents will turn out to be relevant to your poetry, but give it time to find its place. For many years, I was ambivalent about my interest in cooking. Cooking ability often translates into added labor, especially for women—labor that is generally unseen and repetitive and done at the cumulative expense of writing time. Eventually, my interest in food became a cornerstone of my writing life.

AM: What are you working on now? What creative pursuits most excite you, today?

AS: Lately I've been writing prose, including a piece on children's books for *New Ohio Review*; a short piece for the Instagram page *Apparel for Authors* (June 12, 2021); and another short piece on AAPI Heritage Month for *USA Today* (May 17, 2021). I'm working on a longer essay on Chinese restaurants. Poetry is still my main genre, but this moment in history seems also to be calling for prose. As when I first read poems that moved me, I remain the most excited by creative works that elicit a visceral response; I wish I could generalize about what constitutes such works, but it's a gut response, an understanding one feels rather than thinks.

2021

Interview with Mihaela Moscaliuc
for *Plume*, 2021

MM: *Peach State* delights at every level. I fell in love right away with its tastes, aromas, and textures, and with the poems' insistence on naming them all with almost devotional precision. I remember how, while reading the rosemary, sage, raspberry, tomato, and "Chinese parsley" poems of *Living Quarters,* I craved more, so I got excited as soon as I saw the pre-pub description of *Peach State*.

The culinary and sensory feast to which we are treated here is also more than that. *Peach State* delights as much as it instructs, in the best sense of the word. Embedded in its poems one finds insights into Chinese culinary traditions and their place in your family's history in Atlanta, with anecdotes that illuminate the complexities of assimilation and acculturation. There are also poems (including "That Almond Dessert," "On the Recommendation That American Adults Consume No More Than One Quarter Cup of Rice, Twice a Week," "Xiaolongbao," "Name That Restaurant") that hold a mirror up to the dominant culture's failure to do *its* part, the superficiality with which it (mis)appropriates, misnames, tokenizes. All this is done with tenderness and sometimes humor. How did these intertwined conversations about food, identity, place, and belonging emerge? Was it poem by poem? Did you anticipate, from the beginning, that what might start in passion for one thing might take you on so many intersecting journeys?

AS: Thank you for this thoughtful question, and for connecting the two books. The answer is a little of everything. I had a broad sense of what I wanted *Peach State* to do, but many of the realizations and asides emerged poem by poem. Many times, I went around Atlanta juxtaposing what I saw with what I remembered from childhood. My daughters and I would go to Kung Fu Tea on Buford Highway and see it bustling with Asian customers and employees, and I'd marvel that when I was their age, you almost never bumped into another Asian person in a café—and in those days all the cafés gestured toward Europe, bubble tea was unknown, and Buford Highway was just a road. I knew that writing about food had tremendous potential but had no idea how far it could go; I don't think I realized how useful the language of cookbooks and cooking instruction could be, nor did I expect to have so much fun with the language of eating. I also discovered that there is a lot of Chinese American food vocabulary, and that a fair amount of it resides in mainstream American discourse.

MM: Food holds memories, and writing about it can become a means of recovering the past or a history (with all its truths and myths) to which we have lost full access. Food activates nostalgia, and it may be also a way of staving off the process of forgetting, or of forgetting who we are, who we have become. I am thinking of "Black Sesame" in particular, but many of the poems do important work of "excavation." Did the writing of any of these poems surprise you with memories you did not know you had?

AS: Yes! I had forgotten many small things, simply from not seeing them for many years, since they had fallen out of fashion or were no longer needed: canned fruit cocktail; hot dogs as a stand-in for Chinese sausage; ginger slices preserved in sherry. And while substitutions may have seemed like stopgap measures to the first generation, those foods were creating memories for that generation's children, who experienced the food on their plates, not the food in someone else's mind. I had also forgotten the Chinese carvings made of olive or peach pits, which returned for me late in the project, when the repeating motif of peaches prompted me to consider more modes in which the peach appears.

MM: I too had forgotten about the exquisite art form of pit-carving until reading "My Life in Peaches," in which you mention the "tiny carvings / in tiny pits— // Buddhas, houses, / forests, fish." Looking at the stunning pit carvings of some Chinese masters I wondered about parallels to poetic craft, and specifically to the craft of your poems. The raw material into which the poems are carved—subjects such as food, cooking, family, language, tradition—is sometimes as ordinary as fruit pits, but what you do with the material and within various constraints (line by line, stanza by stanza) to render such material malleable and surprising, is extraordinary. *Peach State*'s cornucopia of forms contains the villanelle, the ghazal, the sestina, the sonnet, along with poems of various stanzaic structures and prosodic scales, including pieces that lean toward prose poetry and lyrical essays (or zuihitsu?), such as "Wakefulness" and "When I Said I Grew Up Speaking No Chinese, I Was Forgetting These Words." How do you see the relation between form and content? Did some of these poems find/call for their structure right away? Any examples of poems that were more reluctant and underwent experimentation?

AS: Usually, the form emerges during the writing process; I seldom know what it's going to be ahead of time. But "The Chow-Mein Years in Atlanta" had "villanelle" written all over it from the start. "Wakefulness" is secretly a sestina. It didn't work in the traditional stanzas. The queen of sestinas, Sandra Beasley, helped me see that it would function better if formatted as a prose poem. I'm thrilled that you see so many possible names for the form of "When I Said I Grew Up Speaking No Chinese, I Was Forgetting These Words";

I imagined it as a satirical glossary or "ingredients" section at the front or back of a cookbook.

MM: One of my favorite pieces is "Everything That Can Be Eaten," which is a feast in itself (that makes me hungry even when I'm full), but also an ode to resourcefulness, and maybe an ars poetica of sorts? (This might be a personal favorite because it also returns me to those "hunger" days in Romania when we learned not only to survive on potatoes, beans, and cabbage, but found so many ways to cook them, it never got boring.)

I'm quoting the beginning here so readers may "taste" it, but also as a way of asking you about cadence and music, both of which come from multiple sources in your poems, including alliteration, assonance, and playful internal and end rhyming. There's the perfect *hunger-shoulder* and *diagonal-animal*, but also the internal *cut* and chest*nut*, the subtle chiming of *lo mein—broccoli stem—can*, the *stir-fries* and *undersized*, and more. Do you make most of these choices about soundwork/the poem's soundscape in the process of drafting, or in the process of revision? What are the most exciting and/or challenging ways of making your lines sing?

> Thus my peripatetic starving-artist years passed without
>   hunger.
> The always-unpopular chicken thighs and pork shoulder,
>
> combined with an untranslatable pantry and daily effort,
> made me richer, though unemployed, than an assistant
>   professor.
>
> Tofu, ruined for most by baking, quadrupled the meat in
>   stir-fries.
> No. 9 thin spaghetti could be lo mein, otherwise found in
>   undersized

pouches under "ethnic." Peeled broccoli stems, cut on the
    diagonal,
had the crispness of water chestnuts, minus the can. Picked
    animal

bones could be simmered into broth; to discard them was
    a crime.
Yesterday's rice, fried with frozen peas, an egg, and yesterday's
    ham,

made lunchtime new. (...)

AS: I love that this poem brought back for you a time in your life
in Romania with culinary parallels. In my process, choices about
sound occur in both phases, but they're more accidental or unconscious in the early drafting stage. Revision is where sound is more
deliberate—but not entirely, since much of revision is looking at
the messy drafts and finding sound correspondences that seemed
to have happened spontaneously. I think the most exciting *and*
challenging aspect of sound is that not everyone agrees on what
constitutes rhyme. I've been accused of writing unrhymed poems
that I thought were rhymed, or semi-rhymed. But in the end, does
what we call it matter?

MM: Poet Michael Waters once asked Maxine Kumin if she had a
name for rhyming the final word of one line with the internal syllable of a following or preceding line. He captures the moment in his
poem "Elegy with Strawberries":

I asked Max, still swimming in her poem,
If there was a name for the device
In rhymed couplets of slanting

The final word of one line
With the internal syllables of the next.

Dipping the nippled fruit
Into its saucer of powdered sugar,
She tensed her brow in concentration,
Yes, she grinned, pleased
With her answer: _Desperation!_

Maxine found form and formal gestures freeing. "The tougher the form," she said, "the easier it is for me to handle the poem, because the form gives permission to be very gut honest." Do you find form freeing? Do you have any name for your ingenious rhyming?

AS: Maxine Kumin is in my pantheon. I love the name she uses and how Michael Waters captures it in his poem! I've never thought to name my own means of rhyming and am honored that you think it might deserve one. If I had to think of a name, I might suggest "approximation" or "echoing"—though "desperation" is about as accurate as it gets.

I feel a keen affinity with Kumin's ideas about form: I too find it freeing. I do it as much for the writing process as for the product—maybe even more for the process. Having to rhyme or repeat at set points stops me from moving too logically from one point to the next; it prompts more leaping, more remote association, more surprise.

MM: Is there a poem in _Peach State_ that feels particularly important to you because of its content, function in the collection, the process of writing it, or for other reasons?

AS: The first, "Substitutions," or the last, "An Hour Later, You're Hungry Again," might be one of those. Their images capture some quality about family life that felt, in my early life, eternal and repeating. *Peach State* is a prolonged effort to fight the possibility that it is (was) not eternal.

MM: Do you think of *Peach State* as (also) poetry of place?

AS: Yes! Some part of me never left my hometown, yet when I go there, I feel like both "stranger and native." When I'm away, it takes on the imaginative potential created by having to fill in the details that don't present themselves.

MM: What are you working on at the moment? The issue in which this interview/conversation appears will also feature 5-6 new poems. If you already have some of them, would you share a few words about the source of inspiration, what excites you about them, or anything else you see fit?

AS: It's hard to generalize at this point, but they are poems about loss or potential loss. Maybe all poems are, but I'm driven at this moment to think about memory: not just the way it functions—as a mixture of recalling and imagining—but also how it operates in the context of migration and illness (memory loss). Dementia is a terrible disease with pockets of mercy; migration always involves the memory of one or the other country; my family has been affected by both. As students, most of us wish for photographic memory, but in life, it's important to be able to forget some things.

MM: Your poems ("Doughnuts" among them) mention daughters. I know poetry is not autobiography (something I learned from my first teacher, Ilya Kaminsky, whom I asked, within minutes of meeting, how his son—the son I'd read about in a poem—was. He laughed kindly and said he had no son, and that was our first lesson about poetry), but if you do have children: How do you see the relationship between parenting and writing? Do you see writing as another way of preserving and passing on a heritage that records narratives of origin but also narratives of transformation, of cultural alchemy?

AS: That's a useful anecdote! Family members who appear in my poems are to some extent fictionalized, as is the persona of the speaking "poet."

One major difference between parenting and writing is the relationship to time. Parenting, especially when children are young, is immediate and all about action—though you do have to be careful what you say because it can be misheard and/or make a lasting impression. Writing is about the long term, beyond the writer's lifetime, one hopes, and while you also have to be careful what you say, you also have to be *less* careful; it's important to have a degree of abandon, of getting past "what will people think of me?" and imagining the day everyone you know no longer walks on this earth.

When I started writing, I was too young to imagine myself as a parent, but now I can see writing as you describe it in the last question. Poems can operate like family photographs, recording what you so aptly call "narratives of origin," but the power of poetry is that the faces in the photographs, the surroundings, the circumstances, change according to the reader, even—especially—when the poem makes those things specific.

2021

Interview with Elizabeth Marie Bolaños
for *The Adroit Journal*, 2021

EB: *Peach State* is ripe with food's connection to your identity, a theme that lives in much of your previous work, too. Have you ever created a meal solely inspired by a special moment in your life?

AS: There was a time when I put together abundant meals, often with unfamiliar recipes, on the slightest pretext, for fun: in graduate school and other "starving artist" circumstances, I was always having dinner parties. Then one day, all at once, I had a full-time teaching job and a newborn. Holiday meals and birthday cakes had no leeway for disasters, so for officially "special" days when my children were very young, I favored the tried and true. Still, it wasn't long before even they were up for trying something new, such as a birthday cake piled with homemade marshmallows (I can't take credit for that recipe). In any case, time-management challenges have taught me, more generally, not to be over-invested in how things turn out. Some of the most joyful and imaginative cooking arises from making what you can from what happens to be on hand. Homemade pizza does this well, as you can make a smattering of vegetable bits, leftover meat, cured things from jars (artichokes, olives), and odds and ends of cheese into a dinner that looks and tastes intentional. Cooking and writing are similar in this way: it goes best when you're not under pressure to perform; if you practice enough, once you let go of the idealized result, it takes off.

EB: You explore food in layers that feel tangible, as if each poem is edible with its own unique flavors. I felt the bittersweet ones lingered with me the longest. Do you ever feel this way when writing, as if you're composing a meal?

AS: I appreciate this notion of eating the poem, with bitter and sweet balancing each other out. You've reminded me of the many ways writing parallels the composition of a meal, where you need a balance of flavors, textures, colors, boldness, and neutrality, and it all has to make nutritional sense. Most home cooks have inadvertently produced a beige dinner—mashed potatoes, broiled cod, and steamed cauliflower—that's perfectly nourishing and even delicious but visually comic, a little off-putting. You don't go back and revise the meal—you laugh and have dinner and that's the end of it. In writing, you not only get to revise, you have to, because that poem may be served over and over to who knows how many people. There probably is some synesthesia to revising, an intuitive moment when the poem generates, for instance, the right color, texture, heat level (in temperature or spice), or feeling of having had a good meal. Pulling the poem into its finished shape is like identifying the missing element for a salad: the orange pepper or pickled onion or slivered pear that meets not only a flavor, smell, or texture requirement but also a visual one, because eating, when you pay attention, is an aesthetic experience as well as a functional one.

EB: I love the line "Our story began when my parents arrived as immigrants," from the poem "Personal History." Was the idea for the book inside you for a while, brought upon gradually, suddenly?

AS: Miraculously, it was there, waiting for me to find it. Once I identified it, by writing a sabbatical proposal, a gate opened. I had a better perspective on my previous poems as well; they had been circling this book without my explicit knowledge. Of course, the actual writing still took a long time, and assembling the final manuscript was the same struggle it always is, but I could see parts of the whole coming together sooner than with previous books.

EB: Did you visit Georgia while creating this collection? Or do any traveling for that matter?

AS: Whenever I could. It was in large part to see my parents and other relatives, but every visit also renewed my perspective on early experiences and helped me imagine my parents' lives there before I was born. As a teenager, I sometimes resented that our restaurant-going skewed so heavily Chinese, when restaurants of all kinds were opening in Atlanta. I wanted to try the foods of more countries. But my maternal grandparents were living in Atlanta then, and while they loved a good steakhouse, they often chose the restaurant for us all. My grandfather was effusive about food in a way that perhaps shows up in my voice on the page; he loved to narrate, like a sportscaster, as dishes arrived, and he photographed the food, long before photo-taking became free and easy. Returning to that landscape, where the restaurants have multiplied and attracted national attention, prompts me to remember and imagine. I'm speaking in terms of when I was writing the book. Today, after over a year without travel and with immense challenges for restaurants, I worry about how that landscape will look when I can visit again. As background work for *Peach State,* my mother and I would occasionally drive by the shells of closed restaurants we used to frequent as a family. One day we parked in front of one of the oldest, of which I had only a vague visual memory, and tried to imagine the modest building—it had become a Thai restaurant—

in its old incarnation. I was so young in its day that without my mother, I wouldn't have been able to find it. Other trips included New York, where I visited food exhibits at the Museum of Chinese in America and the Museum of Food and Drink, and San Francisco, where I was doing readings from *Living Quarters* but also took the chance to see family friends, who shared some of the early scenarios in *Peach State*.

EB: One of my favorite poems is "When I Said I Grew Up Speaking No Chinese, I Was Forgetting These Words." Can you tell me a little about the process for creating this one?

AS: Thank you for liking it! Much of the background work for *Peach State* involved immersion in cookbooks, many of which were quirkily indexed. Browsing them was great, but when I wanted to look up something specific, dishes and ingredients became elusive, even in some books with rigorous indexing. I realized that I had never known what certain foods were called, or I had learned only an approximate name for them. Regionalisms, romanizations, and pronunciations—never mind translations—were all over the place, and it wasn't just me: there was no consensus on what to call them. My own parents, who grew up speaking different dialects of Chinese, might each have a different name for the same food, and a family friend who grew up speaking yet another dialect might have still another name for it. As a result, some of the foods I was trying to remember were effectively hidden, even—sometimes especially—from an internet search. That even a person who grew up eating these foods (a poet, whose medium is language) could not definitively name them gnawed at me. In childhood you trust that older generations can keep track, but later you realize that older generations won't always be around.

EB: Some of the poems unearth racial issues which still poison society today, but you educate the ignorant through your lens of experience.

AS: It's gratifying to hear this perspective. When writing, I'm suspicious of any desire on my part to educate, lest the poem turn out didactic, so I go into the process looking for something *I* need to learn. Yet I also feel an urgency about the racial issues you mention and think I would be dishonest not to engage with them.

EB: I love when you talk about food with personification. In the poem "Instant Ramen" for instance, instant ramen was mocked so you wanted to defend it, inform the mockers of its culinary potential.

AS: Thank you! I think the foods we associate with being nurtured as children—if we were fortunate enough to be nurtured—are never entirely inanimate, within our deepest selves. That's one reason it can be so hard to give them up later, if advised to for health or environmental reasons. My hope is that "Instant Ramen" expresses something most people have felt, if not necessarily toward the same food.

EB: Were there any poems you made that you enjoyed but felt shouldn't be included in this collection?

AS: Quite a few poems didn't make the cut. Some were simply weaker than others; some covered the same territory in ways that didn't add enough; others turned out not to fit. Writing those poems wasn't a waste, though: I think of them as part of the drafting process for the book. Only after I started repeating myself could I be sure I'd said all that needed saying; taking redundant poems out is easier than creating missing ones to order. The drawback is that working this way is time-intensive, in a world in which writing time is scarce for all but a very few. Occasionally I write a poem that I later decide shouldn't be published in case it hurts someone, but that's a disappointment. I write to connect with readers and to participate in the conversation among poets.

EB: Is there a poem here you feel especially close to? A heart of the collection maybe? I felt a sense of this in "My Life in Peaches."

AS: This is a terrific question. I haven't previously thought of the poems in this way. I might point to the final poem, "An Hour Later, You're Hungry Again," as reflective of a family ritual that, while it's situated in childhood, speaks to every stage of life and could include everyone in my extended family. It also captures the connection between family and restaurants for many Chinese Americans. But "My Life in Peaches" is more of a distillation of the book, since it invokes images and ideas that occur throughout *Peach State*: suburban grocery stores, the city of Atlanta, the state of Georgia, car culture, Chinese art objects, traditional Southern food, immigrant thrift. It may also be a poem that doesn't stand alone as much as others, as it's so enmeshed in conversation with the rest of the book. In that sense, it may well be the heart.

Interview with Sara London for
Woven Tale Press, 2021

SL: Reading your new book, *Peach State*, made me hungry for authentic Chinese cuisine! Your intimate knowledge of and reverence for the dishes of your forebears (and your contemporaries) is wonderfully recorded in these poems. I love the curiosity and humor with which you chronicle American adulterations of ingredients and names. There's a funny and revealing piece called "The End of Meat," and one of the book's five cookbook-style sections is called "Never Mind, Let's Go Out." Did you initially set out to write a book of poems about food?

AS: I did, although I wasn't sure what shape it would take. When I started writing *Peach State* in 2015, I was aware that the development of Chinese food in Atlanta paralleled my parents' lives there (over approximately 70 years) and that restaurants and food markets over that period had become a powerful symbol of the city's transformation. I also wanted the early era, even with its more limited food culture, to be remembered. Meanwhile, I've long been interested in food anyway; in a bookstore, I usually go straight to the poetry or cookbook section. Your observations about the poems are gratifying, as I've long hoped to bring together these two passions but was never sure how to do so. Maybe it has finally happened.

SL: It's happened! In "Peaches," you refer to your native Georgia, where, when you were growing up, people asked "*But where are you from originally?*" Your Chinese family were "strangers / and natives on a lonely, beautiful street," and "food came in stackable containers." The poem ends with the image of "typical immigrants' children, / taller than their parents and unaware of hunger / except when asked the odd, perplexing question." Can you talk about the intersection of identity, displacement and poetry in your life?

AS: I grew up in a white suburb, its gleaming supermarkets juxtaposed with my father's accounts of being sent outside, as a teenager, to slaughter a chicken. Eventually I realized that I was perceived as having lived my parents' experiences, even though I was born in Atlanta long after both of them had left China. Much later, I connected this conflation to the absence of the term "Asian American": the closest word we had was "Oriental." Mostly, the term was "Chinese" or "Korean" or whatever one's ancestry was, which naturally leads a child to think she *is* Chinese or Korean. I loved writing creatively and had little difficulty expressing myself in words. But when it came to describing my own family and the small, scattered Chinese American community I knew, the vocabulary was missing. In high school, my fictional characters were white, my poems' speakers racially unspecific—neither of which is categorically wrong, but it was unexamined. In retrospect, that was a form of displacement, though emigration (along with poor U.S.-China relations) was the more obvious displacement. Luckily I was headed toward poetry anyway, the art of attempting to name what eludes naming.

SL: Sometimes, even for the poet, language itself can be elusive. In addition to mentioning linguistic elements like "muddled" nomenclature (referenced comically in "That Almond Dessert"), you allude, in some poems, to your own sense of inadequacy with the

Chinese language. As an English-language writer, are there ways you've felt restrained linguistically? Has your knowledge of Chinese given you any notable insights about English?

AS: I love studying languages and took courses in so many (Latin, French, Italian, Chinese, Japanese) that I am master of none. I invested the most in Chinese and was briefly at ease in it conversationally, though with limited reading skill and no ability to discuss special topics (except maybe food!). But having encountered so many languages' music and grammar, I do at times feel the limitations of English. Its tenses eliminate ambiguities of time that are possible in Chinese, which conveys time through context rather than conjugation. I seldom write in syllabics because I'm aware that syllable counts work better in Japanese. And a colleague told me about a classical Chinese form that one-ups the English palindrome poem by being readable forward and backward, character by character, rather than line by line. I wish I were equipped to even translate such a poem! And then, more obviously, the visual dimension of Chinese isn't available in English. That said, some Chinese American poets are using characters in English-language poems. Although I haven't done it myself, I'm interested in the possibilities it opens up.

SL: A number of your poems utilize fixed forms—villanelles, sonnets, sestinas, ghazals. One of the poems (soon to be) in WTP is written in a Spanish form called glosa. How consciously, and why, do you decide to use repetition and/or rhyme in a given poem? Did the formal poems in the book begin, in their earliest drafts, with strict form?

AS: Few began with form. Most of my poems begin as amorphous free-writes that I later sift through in search of the seed of something less messy. Usually, words or lines emerge that have the potential to provide structure; preoccupations show up and gesture toward certain forms. At that point I consciously consider what form can support what the poem seems to want to do. Exceptions: "The Chow-Mein Years in Atlanta" announced itself right away as a villanelle, but it may be an outlier because I was responding to a nearly overnight call for submissions from the Asian American Writers Workshop. The post-*Peach State* glosa arose in response to a form-specific prompt from Kelli Russell Agodon and Martha Silano's *The Daily Poet,* a book that helped end a silence that had accompanied the first six months or so of the pandemic. Regardless of when in the process they appear, forms help me know when a poem is finished; they provide reasons to choose one of two or more words that in free verse might work equally well.

SL: And since we're still in the midst of a protracted pandemic, how have your passions for poetry and food served you during these past many months?

AS: I've been immensely grateful to have cooking skills and to have been a community-supported agriculture subscriber for so long, which trained me to let the ingredients determine the meal, even if you saw a lot of the same vegetable week after week. (It took years to reverse the suburban habit of picking dishes I wanted to cook, generating a shopping list from the recipes, and filling a cart with little regard for season.) Last spring, when no one was sure how risky it was to go to the grocery store and local farms were not yet producing, I was able to buy storage vegetables from the Dickinson College Farm and enjoy, say, a profusion of potatoes. In late summer, I canned a lot of tomatoes. As I mentioned earlier, poetry writing was not available to me early in the pandemic, but designing online courses in poetry kept me nourished, and now writing is possible again. As a poet, I've always had spells of silence, during which I'm simply observing. The pandemic may have coincided with the natural silence that sometimes follows the completion of a book. It's hard to tell.

INTERVIEW WITH WENDY INGERSOLL PERRY
FOR *QUARTET JOURNAL*, 2022

WP: Adrienne, in your poems you utilize such diverse topics as food, language/words, girlhood/womanhood, to serve as vehicles to explore your family's immigration to the United States from China before your birth. In particular many of your poems address finding a home in this country in which you were born, while simultaneously being homesick for a place in which you have never lived. "Illumination" (*Middle Kingdom*) beautifully illustrates not only this particular in-between state, but the in-between state of being sixteen years old, when you "knew that if things had happened differently, / I could disappear among them..." Did you start writing about assimilation at a young age, or as an adult looking back? Tell us a bit about your journey.

AS: Thank you for reading with care all the way back to my first book! It wasn't until college that I gained the vocabulary and perspective to start writing about race and assimilation. In childhood, as one of few Asian Americans in the community, I was at once keenly aware of racial difference and completely helpless to talk or write about it. I was about eleven when my father took his first trip in over thirty years back to his native China—a dramatic journey, but one whose significance I didn't understand. In college, I took courses on Chinese language, history, and thought, mainly out of a desire to fill the gaps in my Eurocentric secondary education. I knew I wanted to be a writer and kept meaning to take English courses, but one Chinese-language course leads to another, and meanwhile, I was drawn to other previously unavailable subjects, including the study of religion, most memorably, a course called "The Sacred Geography of Traditional China." Imagining China had always been a part of my consciousness; to imbue actual places on a map with sanctity was irresistible to the poet in me. The trade-off is that I had little formal education in literature in English. I wish I could have gone to college twice.

The moment described in "Illumination" was, as I remember it, an ars poetica moment, but in the context of *Middle Kingdom*, the poem and therefore the episode become layered with other meanings, including the racial inability to "disappear among" the other kids. Maybe this is one of the reasons poems are seldom true to "what really happened."

WP: At first glance, many of your poems appear free in form, and there is often a lovely casual tone, as if the speaker is sharing confidences with a friend. On second reading the reader perceives not only skillful formal aspects, but frequent and subtle rhyme—interior and end-rhyme, true and off-rhyme. There is magic in how you use these tools to explore "in-between-ness." For example, in "The Jews of Kaifeng" (*Peach State*), you use end rhymes such as matzah/Buddha and Center/forever. Did you have a sonnet in mind from the first draft, or did that underpinning come forward later in the revision process? And I'm also wondering what is your process for choosing rhyme—do you use a rhyming dictionary or does rhyme just spring from your brain as you write?

AS: I appreciate your attention to those rhymes and off-rhymes. I had no idea "The Jews of Kaifeng" was going to be a sonnet. Its first couple of drafts were long and rambling. Rarely do I know ahead what form a poem is going to take, even when it ends up in a received form as tight as the sonnet. But the more practice I get with forms, the more readily I can see them emerging.

The rhyming dictionary is my place of last resort. If my brain refuses to produce the word with the desired meaning and sound, I go to the thesaurus; the nuances of meaning laid bare in the thesaurus often generate associated words, one of which might have the right sound. But if the thesaurus fails, I'll use the rhyming dictionary in the hope that it will jog something. Still, it's often a meandering search, since I have such an affection for off-rhyme, and rhyming dictionaries seldom provide off-rhymes.

Of course, the overall hope is that in the end, the line sounds as if were naturally occurring, and not labored, despite the labor it required.

WP: Many of your poems contain low-key and clever humor and irony. For example, in "1978" (*Middle Kingdom*), the speaker looks back on her youth: "we crunch ice cubes and jeer the veins / in a mother's calves. We don't mean / to be mean, but...we know / we'll soon be swollen and blue / and white ourselves, so now's / the time." The poem reveals sorrow behind its jaunty tone, heartbreak inherent to that confusing time of life, taking the reader to unexpected places. How did you choose to use humor to write about serious subjects?

AS: If I set out to be funny, I will fail. I think writing comedy requires a whole other brand of imagination. But when writing about serious subjects, the occasional funny thing crops up. Maybe it's easier to be funny when the mood is somber because no one is expecting it. Some of the most deeply felt laughter occurs at funerals. I don't plan it; I think junctures arise in a poem where some kind of relief is needed, and the moment of levity presents itself. Ideally, as well-deployed humor does, it simultaneously heightens the serious feeling.

WP: You display a great talent for astonishing endings—I was again and again stunned by them. The poem "The End of Meat" (*Peach State*) is an example: a reference to a Chinese cookbook begins "many thoughtful and educated people, citing health, the environment, or / the rights of animals, have given it up" but concludes "I try to view the end as a beginning, / a place where you reset your point of reference...and build from the erasure, as if leaving one country for good, then reaching / another." Are these poetic destinations unexpected by you as well, or do you start with an idea and work backwards—in other words, in your writing do you build stairs or do you let yourself fall down them?

AS: Thank you for all of this generous reading. I love the stair metaphor. The answer is the second: to reach the end of a poem, I have to let myself "fall down them." It's hard to do; life is full of situations over which you have to exert control. And I do have long stretches of silence, during which it's easy to think I'll never finish another poem—more likely, end up at the bottom of a staircase with bumps and bruises. But as long as I keep putting words on paper, I've found that eventually, the "poetic destination" comes into sight.

An Hour Later, You're Hungry Again

For the table to be round.
For the teapot to be bottomless.
For your elders to compose the menu.

For the waiter to recite the order back.
For the fish-maw soup to be ladled at the table.
For red vinegar to bloom in it, a submerged flower.

For the bright lights and immaculate tablecloth.
For the extra order of Singapore noodles.
For the white blossoms on Chinese broccoli.

For your mother to warn you which sauces are hot.
For your brother to turn the lazy Susan just when you need it.
For the cloth napkin to slide to the floor.

For rice in a hexagonal lacquered box.
For the hill of bones on your tiny plate.
For the Wash 'n Dri packet after the lobster.

For the sea bass to give up its spine without resistance.
For your aunt to serve you nameless meats you love.

For your grandfather to assign everyone a favorite dish,
    incorrectly.

For the shrimp to have expressionless eyes.
For your grandmother to murmur "thank you" as everyone
    serves her.
For the owner to insist on calling your father "professor."

For the ice water you requested but forgot to drink.
For the film of oil on your last grains of rice.
For the gift of red bean soup with the oranges.

For the numbers on the check, in Chinese penmanship.
For the leftovers in their cartons, in tied plastic bags.
For the Chinese-newspaper rack in the vestibule.

For night to have fallen while you were eating.
For ginger and scallions to infiltrate the dreams
from which you will wake in the only home you know.

CREDITS:

Maxine Kumin, "Looking Back in My Eighty-First Year," *Still to Mow,* Norton, 2007 (68-69).

Li-Young Lee, excerpt from "The Cleaving" from *The City in Which I Love You* (Rochester: BOA Editions Ltd., 1990) (included in a review of Dorothy Wang, *Thinking Its Presence: Form, Race, and Subjectivity in Contemporary Asian American Poetry* (Redwood City, California: Stanford University Press, 2014) (2018)

Molly Peacock, "So What If I Am in Love," Original Love, Norton, 1995 (22-23).

Adrienne Rich, excerpt from "Prospective Immigrants, Please Note" from *Collected Poems: 1950-2012* Copyright © 2016 by the Adrienne Rich Literary Estate. Copyright © 1967, 1963 by Adrienne Rich. Used by permission of W. W. Norton & Company, Inc.

Adrienne Su, "Middle Kingdom," and "Address" from *Middle Kingdom* (New Gloucester, ME: Alice James Poetry Collective, 1998).

Adrienne Su, "Substitutions," "That Almond Dessert," and "An Hour Later, You're Hungry Again," from *Peach State: Poems* (Pittsburgh, Pennsylvania: University of Pittsburgh Press, 2021). Reprinted with permission of publisher.

Adrienne Su, "Wedding Gifts" from *Sanctuary* (2006). Published by Manic D Press: San Francisco. Reprinted with permission of publisher.

Adrienne Su, excerpt from "Sestina" from *Having None of It* (2009). Published by Manic D Press: San Francisco. Reprinted with permission of publisher.

Adrienne Su, excerpts from "Illumination" and "1978" from *Middle Kingdom* (New Gloucester, ME: Alice James Poetry Collective, 1997).

Michael Waters, excerpt from "Elegy with Strawberries" from *Sinnerman* (Wilkes-Barre, Pennsylvania: Etruscan Press, 2023) (included in an interview with Mihaela Moscaliuc for *Plume* (2021))

ADRIENNE SU is the author of five books of poems, most recently *Peach State*, which was named a 2022 Book All Georgians Should Read. Her poems appear in many anthologies, including six volumes of *The Best American Poetry*. Among her awards are an NEA fellowship and residencies at the Virginia Center for the Creative Arts, Yaddo, and The Frost Place. An Atlanta native, she lives in Carlisle, Pennsylvania, where she is professor of creative writing at Dickinson College.